An Oxford University Chest

An Oxford University Chest

John Betjeman

Illustrated in line and half-tone by
L. MOHOLY-NAGY,
OSBERT LANCASTER, THE REV. EDWARD BRADLEY
and others

Oxford   New York   Toronto   Melbourne
OXFORD UNIVERSITY PRESS
1979

Oxford University Press, Walton Street, Oxford OX2 6DP

OXFORD LONDON GLASGOW
NEW YORK TORONTO MELBOURNE WELLINGTON
KUALA LUMPUR SINGAPORE JAKARTA HONG KONG TOKYO
DELHI BOMBAY CALCUTTA MADRAS KARACHI
NAIROBI DAR ES SALAAM CAPE TOWN

First published by John Miles 1938.
First issued as an Oxford University Press paperback 1979.
Reprinted 1979.

British Library Cataloguing in Publication Data

Betjeman, Sir John
An Oxford University Chest.
1. University of Oxford – History
2. University of Oxford – Buildings
I. Title
378.425'74   LF521

ISBN 0-19-281273-4

Printed in Great Britain by
Hazell Watson & Viney Ltd,
Aylesbury, Bucks

TO

MY MOTHER

CONTENTS

LIST OF ILLUSTRATIONS

List of Illustrations

List of Illustrations

ACKNOWLEDGMENTS

All the photographs in this book were taken by L. Moholy-Nagy, except for those facing pages 7, 145 and 152, which were by Miss Joan Eyres Monsell, and that facing page 18, which is by Will F. Taylor, and that facing page 137 is by Miss Yvonne Howard. The drawings on pages 14, 16, 19, 25, 27, 30, 35, 37, 39, 40, 41, 57, 82 and 96 are by Osbert Lancaster, all the rest in the main text of the book are by the Rev. Edward Bradley ("Cuthbert Bede"), author of *The Adventures of Mr. Verdant Green* and *Little Mr. Bouncer*, from which books the illustrations are taken. The engraving on page 126 is from *The New Pocket Companion for Oxford*, 1802; the pen and wash drawing on page 26 is from *Aspects of Modern Oxford* by "A Mere Don"; all other drawings and engravings are from Ingram's *Memorials of Oxford* (three volumes, 1837).

The author wishes to express his gratitude to Mr. Ernest F. Marsh for contributing a paper on his life at Oxford, to Mr. G. A. Kolkhorst, M.A., to Professor Geoffrey Webb of Cambridge for information on the work of Wren at Oxford, to Father Ronald Knox, to Mr. Neville Coghill, M.A., to Mr. M. Platnauer, M.A., to Mr. L. Rice Oxley, M.A., to Mr. W. T. Coxhill, F.I.S.A., to the former Warden of Wadham, the late Principal of Brasenose, the former President of Trinity, the Rector of Lincoln, the Dean

Acknowledgments

of Christ Church, the President of Magdalen, Mr. H. W. House, M.A., Mr. J. H. A. Sparrow, M.A., to a reader of the Oxford University Press who looked over the proofs with an expert eye, the former Warden of Merton, the President of St. John's, Bodley's Librarian, Dr. Plant of the University Museum, Professor H. G. Fiedler of the Taylor Institution, Mr. J. N. Bryson, M.A., the late Provost of The Queen's College, the Provost of Worcester, all of whom gave help, information or permission to take photographs. Finally he would like to thank Mr. H. F. Paroissien, for his patience and assistance in the production of this book, Mr. John Bury and the Curators of the Oxford University Chest also deserve thanks. Many Oxford friends helped the author with conversation and suggestions, and he hopes they will take this, the only intimation, of his sincere thanks. But Mr. J. W. Gynes must be thanked personally for his generous and valuable advice on Oxford affairs.

Chapter One

THE THREE OXFORDS

There are three Oxfords, Christminster, Motopolis and the University.

I

Christminster is the market town of Hardy's *Jude*, a place to which country people come to find work and where farmers still try to do business. Christminster lies for the most part to the west of Oxford between the canal and the University. Its old cattle market has lately been translated into a car-park, but there is a corn merchants' down by the canal and in Queen Street and in the little side streets in St. Ebbe's you will still see shops which sell oil lamps, wicks, and agricultural implements. In these parts too you will find cheap furniture for sale not only of the jazz modern sort (upholstered leather, shot silk, and Birmingham brassware) but second-hand stuff that does not interest even the most sophisticated antique hunter—painted firescreens, writhing vases, cumbersome clocks such as might deck the parlour of some small farm among the elms ten or twenty miles away.

THE OXFORD CREDIT SYSTEM

The houses of Christminster are of two sorts. The older ones are gabled and covered with plaster washed yellow. Here and there behind the main streets you may come across Christminster pubs with country people in them. Down in High Street St. Thomas's, more Christminster's High Street than the famous "High" of the University, some Christminster dwellings still stood up to the latest Housing Acts. In the St. Ebbes district there are many more.

The newer sort of Christminster house is of red brick. It may be plain and a hundred years old, like the houses by the canal bank or it may be genuine early Victorian slum scenery, such as is now used for propaganda purposes. There is the town round the gas works and the town called Jericho behind the University Press. They are typical early industrial settlements such as exist even in market towns unblessed with a university. Here came the people who did not get on in the villages, girls who have taken the wrong path, carpenters with more skill than employment. Here came Jude "the first want being a lodging he scrutinized carefully such localities as seemed to offer on inexpensive terms, the modest type of accommodation he demanded; and after inquiry took a room in a suburb nicknamed 'Beersheba', though he did not know this at the time. Here he installed himself, and having had some tea sallied forth." I have always taken 'Beersheba' to be Jericho. How appropriate it is that Ruskin College, the Labour place of learning ungraciously attached to the University, should be in Walton Street on the very borders of Jericho.

COMMONER, TAILOR AND PARENT

The County Hall, a fine effort in the

Oxford Castle (late Norman.)

Looking on the roof of the Codrington Library towards New College
Chapel, from the Radcliffe Camera.

Norman Style of 1840, glowers down on Christminster. Here are tried crimes for the most part connected with rural life. The County Gaol serves to remind Christminster that its chief overlord is now more the state than the University. In the old days the University was able to humiliate Christminster. "Town and gown" rows were famous. Ever since St. Scholastica's day 1354 when sixty-two scholars were killed by men of Christminster, until 1825 the Mayor, Bailiffs and sixty citizens came to the University Church of St. Mary's and deposited sixty-two pence there as a penance. And twenty-nine years after that the Corporation still took an oath to keep the privileges of the University. Well within living memory there have been fights between undergraduates and "townees" and indeed an Oxford novelist of the 'sixties uses one of these fights as an important part of the plot.*

There are still a few aged clergymen, schoolmasters and retired professors spending their last years in the quiet bicycle-haunted, laburnum-shaded roads of North Oxford who refer contemptuously to Christminster men as "townies" and recall the fights of their undergraduate days. There are still townsmen who are none too pleased to see an ex-University man taking part in civic life. But most of the men of Christminster have shaken hands with those of the University. As fields become pasture, as barns decay, as farmers are ruined and taxed, as the horse gives place to the lorry, as the milk goes to the co-operative dairy, as the food is shaken out of the tin, as the co-ops flourish,

UNIVERSITY SERMON

* *The Mysteries of Isis.* 1866.

3

and as the multiple stores distribute their free gifts, so Christminster the market town decays, and another, more sinister community takes its place.

Once a year Christminster comes into its own. When the dons are away with their families, when the undergraduates are in the Cotswolds and the Pyrenees at reading parties, when college porters are making a bit shewing Americans round the chapel, St. Giles' fair begins.

It is about the biggest fair in England. The whole of St. Giles and even Magdalen Street by Elliston and Cavell's right up to and beyond the War Memorial, at the meeting of the Woodstock and Banbury roads, is thick with freak-shows, roundabouts, cake-walks, the whip, and the witching waves. Every sort of fairman finds it worth his while to come to St. Giles'. Old roundabouts worked by hand that revolve slow enough to suit the very young or the very old, ageing palmists and sinister, alluring houris excite the wonder and the passions of red-faced ploughmen.

From the top of the wooden tower, mat in hand, waiting my turn, I have surveyed the fair where arc lights throw unaccustomed brightness onto St. John's College and the staid Judge's Lodgings, and make the diamond panes of Pusey House twinkle. Beyond St. Giles the University is silent and dark. Even the lights of the multiple stores in the Cornmarket seem feeble. Christminster outshines the other two Oxfords for these two days of the year.

And in the alleys between the booths you can even hear people talking with an Oxfordshire accent, a change from the Oxford one.

Jericho.
Overleaf. MOTOPOLIS, scenes in the Morris works and Oxford's outer suburbs.

II

Christminster was in existence before the University.

An eighth century saint, St. Frideswide, founded her nunnery here and it is possible that her shrine was where the Perpendicular watching chamber now stands in the Cathedral.

Oxford had some strategic importance, for it stands, as Mr. C. R. L. Fletcher says: "On the frontier, as it were, between the Midlands and the South." But it is not an old town. There are no Roman remains and very few Saxon ones. The first mention of Oxford is in 912. It is known that two obscure Saxon kings—Edmund Ironside and Harold Harefoot—died at Oxford and that the Danes and English held a few councils in the town.

The Saxons seemed to have seen the value of a site bounded by water and hills on the east, by bog on the south and west. Only the North and north-west had to be fortified to make the town impregnable. Moreover the site itself was on gravel with clay beneath it. According to Mr. Madan, who knew more about Oxford than most people, the first road into Oxford was at Folly Bridge, down where the college barges are. It seems that the place really did take its old name Oxnaford from a ford for oxen probably at Folly Bridge. Such an easy derivation is a severe blow to the philologists.

As soon as the Normans arrive, we can actually see their ponderous building, and Oxford becomes more than a subject for speculation.

The first Norman Governor, Robert Doilli (1071–c 1120) built the Castle tower and the mound beside it* (from this tower Matilda escaped across the river). His successor probably raised earth ramparts along the North side of the city. These were replaced by stone walls.

---

* According to Mr. Madan in *Oxford Outside the Guidebooks* p. 14, he also built St. Michael's Church in Cornmarket. Other authorities think it earlier. Professor Baldwin Brown in *The Arts in Early England, Vol. II (Anglo-Saxon Architecture)* p. 475, says the tower was never used for defence purposes. He himself quotes Mr. Henry Minn.

5

An All Souls' Quadrangle from the Radcliffe Camera. On the right the Chapel and Hall, on the grass some remains of the Encaenia procession.

He also built the famous Augustinian priory of Osney, near where the stations now stand. Soon Oxford became a typical mediaeval city, full of religious communities, a Jewish quarter and merchants' houses and prickly with steepled churches.

You can still walk beside the fortified part of the mediaeval city. Start at the Castle tower, cross the river by the arty little rock-garden which they have made in place of the old Castle mill.

Turn up Castle Street and take the first alley to your left. This leads across New Road to Bulwarks Lane, another alley opposite, which carries you along behind New Inn Hall Street (in mediaeval days it was known as the Lane of the Seven Deadly Sins, though it now contains almost as many Nonconformist and other Protestant places of worship). In George Street you get mixed up with modern commerce; turn right and walk down to the cross roads. It was about here that the Northgate stood with St. Michael's Church adjoining it. Cross into Broad Street, and you will be following along outside the old city wall. If you turn down the first passage on your right between some shops, you will see a large bit of the old wall still standing among the houses behind the premises of the Oxford Drug Company. This blind courtyard has all the towering gloom one associates with the mediæval parts of Edinburgh.

The city wall carries on down Broad Street, skirting the north of New College and comes out again in hoary glory in New College gardens, where it now forms a nice background for herbaceous borders. In the gardens it takes a turn south to the east of the ancient church of St.-Peter's-in-the-East. If you walk down Holywell into Longwall Street you will find a memory of this walled city again when you come out into the High—this is the Eastgate Hotel. The wall carried on down King Street to Merton Street, and shows itself again as a boundary for Merton Gardens, when it turns West in order to protect Christ Church. It

6

Entrance Porch, St. Mary-the-Virgin's Church, 1637—Oxford's most extravagant Baroque.

crossed St. Aldate's south of Christ Church and ran down Brewer Street where Pembroke College seems to rest on its masonry. In St. Ebbe's Street there was a gate called Littlegate and thence in a few yards West you are back in the Castle.

The boundaries, of course, are of various dates and the wall, ancient as it looks in New College Gardens, and in those parts of the city where its blackened contour juts out of red brick or grey peeling plaster houses, is not of Norman masonry.

Inside the Divinity Schools (c. 1430–1483).

III

MOTOPOLIS

Evening in Oxford was the romantic time. The bells would ring for evening chapel from all the colleges, dim or important, those churches under the influence of the Tractarians would tinkle out a call to even-song, there would be a noise at the boathouses along the Cherwell of punts being moored to the bank and the "plop" of heavy feet walking away along the duckboards, the sun would go down behind the spires and towers, and artists would put the glory into their water-colours, gowned figures would hurry through cloisters, and white choirs would file into the candlelight. The bells would die down, and the University would thank God for another day, well spent, before the serious drinking began.

Now, though the bells ring, you cannot hear them above the motor-bicycles and gear-changing. As for the drinking, it is more often cocoa than vintage port. If ever the victory between town and gown has been decided, it has been decided now. And the victory is with Motopolis. Christminster is no longer a rival to the University, and the University is no longer a rival to Motopolis.

To escapists, to arty people like the author of these pages, the internal combustion engine is, next to wireless, the most sinister modern in-vention. It booms overhead with its cargo of bombs, it roars down the lanes with its cargo of cads, it poisons the air, endangers the streets, deafens the ears and deadens the senses. That its most successful manifestation in England should be at Oxford, of all places, passes belief.

Yet it is so, and the most arty of us must hand it to William Morris the Second. He has given employment to thousands, and money to millions;

8

he has provided a cheap means of transport for hundreds of thousands. No doubt many persons injured by the engine he has helped to popularize have received the expert attention of the Oxford hospitals which he has so munificently endowed. It was only fitting that the University should honour him with a degree, and the country with a peerage.

Yet as the lanes of the country have become blue with the fumes of his success, so have the streets of this University life. And the streets are not only full of fumes. Other commercial enterprises have followed in the wake of the successful motor manufacturer. Speculative builders have run up strips of shoddy houses in almost every country lane around the town. East Oxford, where the works are, beyond Magdalen Bridge, is indistinguishable from Swindon, Neasden, or Tooting Bec. The architectural development of Oxford since the war has completely changed the character of the city.

The college buildings are endangered by motor traffic; main streets are as congested as the Strand; chain-stores have taken the place of small shop-keepers; small gas-lamps have given place to the great lamp-standards; buses have supplanted horse trams; the pale-faced mechanics in Oxford bags and tweed coats, walk down the Cornmarket: the farmers and labourers have disappeared; views are interrupted by motor-cars; open spaces occupied by car-parks; the commercial consistency in shop-front and sign of the last century has been ousted by the competitive garishness in imitation marble, electric light and lettering of big London-controlled enterprises. Oxford is no longer a provincial town. It is a replica of London.

The fate of Oxford has been the fate of most country towns. But there is no doubt that the Morris Motor Works have helped to make the transformation so rapid and complete. Cambridge, for instance, comparatively unblessed by industrialism, still retains its character.

William Morris the Second is not to be blamed for the ruination of

Oxford. The fault lies almost entirely with the Colleges who allowed the land which they owned to become the muddled pretentiousness which passes to-day for a town.

In 1885 William Morris the First, poet, craftsman, Socialist, complained of the vulgarization of Oxford in *The Daily News*. He wrote on behalf of the old houses of the Christminster sort which were then numerous: "Oxford thirty years ago, when I first knew it, was full of these treasures; but Oxford 'culture', cynically contemptuous of the knowledge which it does not know, and steeped to the lips in the commercialism of to-day, has made a clean sweep of most of them; but those that are left are of infinite value, and still give some character above that of Victoria Street or Bayswater to modern Oxford."

But then he had little to complain of except of what his own Gothicizers were doing. Bayswater, certainly, and possibly Victoria Street, have more to be said for them than any of the post-war additions to Oxford. And North Oxford, which is, after all, only the brick and stone expression of the innate suburbanism of modern life, was for those days a neat and spacious bit of planning.

No, the fault lies with the colleges who for the last thirty years have been imbued with a parochialism which does not allow them to peep over their own mellow stone walls. It seems that their estate policy—and the colleges own vast estates from which their incomes are largely derived—has been influenced either by a desire to take no notice of the world outside Oxford, or else to make as much money out of it as is possible. There is, I suppose, no harm in the second policy so long as it is employed with foresight.

I have by me a Whitaker's Almanack for 1933, which gives the income of the Oxford Colleges.

Christ Church and Magdalen and, in a lesser degree, most of the other colleges of Oxford, were large land-owners, according to *Kelly's*

In Old Schools Quadrangle.

Directory for 1887, in just the districts which have been "developed" in the most merciless way round Oxford since then.

Now these colleges are paying for the past stupidity by subscribing to the Oxford Preservation Trust. This trust was founded in 1926 to compete with the jerry-builder. Anyone can see that it was founded sixty years too late. Even now there are enemies in its camp. St. John's College for instance owns parts of Beaumont Street which it intends to demolish. The result cannot fail to be something which puts Worcester College as seen from St. Giles, out of scale and which alters the character of almost the only street in Oxford which compares with Bath or Cheltenham.

You would suppose that Oxford University, the home of culture, the cluster of towers and spires whose fame has spread over five continents, whose portals are entered by reverent students from the older civilizations of the East—you would suppose this little Athens of European civilization, this cradle of toleration and enlightenment, would know something of the principles upon which a town is built.

Until one hundred years ago, the knowledge was still there. The colleges stood among their gardens, bounded by water on the south and east, and by Christminster on the west. To the north were farms. A little foresight, a little application of the innate aptitude for planning possessed by the eighteenth and early nineteenth centuries, would have preserved Oxford for ever.

They could have planned an industrial town, with all their learning, which would have been worthy of the University City beside it. The factories could have been planned away from the dwellings, the dwellings could have been set in green spaces and could have been handsome to look at. Morris Cowley could have been a model for the rest of England, so that visitors to the University, instead of trying to pretend no industrialism was near and bathing themselves in a false twilight of

11

The Clarendon Building (1711–24) on the right,
the Sheldonian (1664–69) on the left.

grey Gothic things, would have naturally hurried to see the living beauty of industrial Oxford after the dead glory of University architecture.

The colleges had it in their power to command good building. They could have been the chief land-owners in the outskirts of the town. The material was there. The genius of William Morris the Second in motor manufacture could hardly have been expected to extend to town-planning. But there were all those books in the Bodleian, all those "first-class brains" churning away in panelled senior common rooms.

You would have thought some concerted action had been possible. You would have imagined that architecture and town-planning had been heard of in the home of culture.

As it is, Oxford remains an unplanned muddle. Motopolis, Christminster and the University are jostled together in hopeless disorder. And if the Radcliffe Square still seems a quiet civic centre for the University, it is because no one has yet had the courage to take down the University Church and turn that desirable site into something more profitable than the alms-box in the South Porch.

In order to understand the callousness which has made Oxford look like what it is, we must turn to the third Oxford which is the University.

IV

UNIVERSITY

The University bursts into mediaeval triumph best at 12 noon on the Wednesday in the ninth week of the Trinity (Summer) Full term, for it is the day and hour of Encaenia (Dedication). Then it is that distinguished statesmen, men of letters, Naval and Military commanders, poets and musicians, are given honorary degrees. Then the Chancellor of the University is himself present and all the dons put on their full Academic dress.

Crazy professors bicycle down from North Oxford to their common-rooms, and struggle into robes which give dignity to the strangest: clergymen Doctors of Divinity, leave their rectories; lawyers leave their dust; musicians their harpsichords and all assemble in the hall of the Vice-Chancellor's college to meet the Chancellor himself, and to partake of the traditional refreshment of peaches and champagne.

I can think of no more appropriate way of unfolding to you the structure of the University than by settling you down to watch the Encaenia procession.

Imagine a blazing day in late June, when the hard light brings out that purple mouldering quality of Oxford stone. You are standing near the Radcliffe Square with the common herd, and never will you feel more common and herded than before this ribbon of learning that will presently come winding by.

At the head of the procession comes the UNIVERSITY MARSHALL carrying a silver wand. He wears a velvet cape and a long broadcloth coat with velvet cuffs and large buttons. On his left arm is a silver badge of the University. His hat is round and squashed with a rosette on it. Normally his duty is to look after the University Police, known as "bull-dogs," who haul delinquent undergraduates before the proctors. On these occasions he wears a bowler hat. He sits in a little office under the Clarendon Building.

His other duties are to ring a hand-bell at University funerals and to look after the seventeen Oxford life-buoys on the river.

COLLEGE LIVING

He is a man of great charm and tact through his duty of "assisting with relations of undergraduates with the Proctors."

Behind the University Marshall come eight BEDELS. In private life they serve the University in some secretarial or clerical capacity. To-day they wear somewhat humbler forms of the dress of the Marshall, with bands. They carry staves. Their sole duty seems to be to announce people on official occasions.

Now comes the CHANCELLOR himself. His robe is black interspersed with twisted gold. Though never Chancellor, I have worn it myself on

Hawksmoor's Twin Gothic Towers, designed early in the eighteenth century, seen from the Radcliffe Camera.

Part of the Encaenia Procession. In the background are typical
"Christminster" houses of a sort now fast disappearing.

a private occasion, and its considerable weight must be irksome in hot weather. The Lord Chancellor of England wears a robe exactly similar except for a gold rosette on each sleeve. The "mortar board" on the Chancellor's head has a gold tassel. He wears bands at his neck. A perfectly ordinary undergraduate in evening-dress carries his train. The undergraduate may be wearing the short undignified commoner's gown which may be seen in the streets any evening of term time.

The rules and regulations of the University are as mysterious as the ceremonial. The Chancellor can only come to Oxford with the permission of the Vice-Chancellor, and then he is only invited as a guest. So the Chancellor of the University is generally some prominent peer whose activities are too numerous to make him visit Oxford often. The first Chancellors of Oxford and of Cambridge were the bishops of the dioceses in which the University was situated. The Chancellor of Oxford University was the Bishop of Lincoln, who was too far off to do much harm.

Next comes the HIGH STEWARD, with the robe or hood of his degree. His is a life-office and there is an obscure Court over which he may preside for trying undergraduates accused of treason, felony and maim. He receives five pounds a year, but looks richer.

Behind the High Steward comes the VICE-CHANCELLOR. He wears the dress of his degree, which may be that of an ordinary M.A. The only thing which distinguishes him will be bands at his neck.

The absence of the chief functionary in the University makes the Vice-Chancellor all-powerful. He is chosen from the heads of colleges by rotation. He holds his office for four years. You may see him during term-time taking his official walks abroad, preceded by a mace-bearer and attendants.

The Vice-Chancellor has a Court over which he has "exclusive and unlimited jurisdiction in all civil cases of action not relating to free-hold."*

The University BURGESSES follow.

Now comes the most colourful part of the procession—the DOCTORS OF THE FACULTIES. You cannot be a "doctor" of the University without first having obtained a Master of Arts degree, unless you are an eminent man given an honorary doctorate. A doctorate is generally the reward for a special thesis written on one's subject.

First come the DOCTORS OF DIVINITY (D.D.). Theology was in mediaeval days the final goal of education so Doctors of Divinity take precedence. Each wears a scarlet robe with sleeves and facings of black velvet, with an edging of alternate crimson and yellow stripes. Beneath the robe is a cassock and cincture, and over it a scarf and bands at the neck. Each wears a hard mortar-board. Doctors of Divinity are mostly old and saintly-looking clergy-men, and their number is decreasing.

Next come the DOCTORS OF MEDICINE (M.D.) in scarlet and blood-crimson with flat Tudor bonnets made of velvet. Behind or before them go the DOCTORS OF CIVIL LAW (D.C.L.) in almost similar robes.

DOCTORS OF LETTERS (D.LITT.) and of SCIENCE (D.SC.) follow in robes of red and French grey. They wear mortar-boards.

Now come the most gorgeous characters of all, the DOCTORS OF MUSIC. They wear robes made of "cream satin brocade with cherry sleeves and facings: the hood is

SOMETIMES PEOPLE NOT CON-NECTED WITH THE UNIVER-SITY ARE GIVEN HONORARY DEGREES

* *Oxford University Ceremonies:* Buxton and Gibson, from whose book much of the information about this procession is culled.

cream brocade with cherry crimson lining. They wear the black laced gown but have no habit."*

Members of the recently created (1917) DOCTORATE OF PHILOSOPHY follow, wearing dark blue robes.

Now you may see the SENIOR and JUNIOR PROCTORS—to the world outside, the most famous characters in the University. They wear black robes made of Russell cord, with silk velvet sleeves and facings of dark blue with red and yellow edgings. Their black silk hoods lined with miniver are turned inside out. To-day is an off-day for the Proctors as they, and the Vice-Chancellor to whom they are responsible, have no powers, because the Chancellor himself is present.†

The Proctors, who hold office for a year, (their office has existed since 1267) and are chosen from among the dons, have no powers at any time inside the walls of colleges, but they find plenty to occupy them in the streets. You may see one or other of the proctors walking about the Oxford streets of an evening during term-time attended by two or more University police, who are men chosen for their athletic prowess. The Proctor wears gown, mortar-board and white tie. The University police —"bulldogs"—wear bowler hats and can run very fast.

It is one of the duties of the Proctors to maintain discipline over and among members of the University in the town. The "bullers" or "bull-dogs" catch delinquent undergraduates, and it is very much like a game of "he." When "he" is caught, he is marched to the proctor, who raises his cap and asks him his name or college. Next day the undergraduate will get a little printed chit asking him to call upon the proctors in the Clarendon building, whose four massive pillars dominate the East end of Broad Street. A usual offence is being out of college after midnight.

* *ibid.*

† There is a story that when the late King Edward VII came to open the Town Hall, the Chancellor was present in his official capacity. When the Chancellor is in his robes, the Vice-Chancellor and his proctors, and the University police have no authority. Many undergraduates got drunk and were clapped into gaol.

There are, of course, various ways of climbing into most colleges, though Wadham, Oriel and Hertford used to be reckoned impregnable. Sometimes undergraduates, living in rooms overlooking the street, have rope-ladders which they let down from their windows for friends. Various public houses have their means of exit. There was one with a ladder hidden in creeper and leading from a bedroom window. There is a tradition, though I have never seen it written in any authoritative work, that the steps of Queen's College and the fender—that is to say the parapet—sheltering the elm trees in front of St. John's College are safe from the Proctors. Some undergraduates having had a row in the High Street were once, it is said, chased by bulldogs to the steps of Queen's College. Here they remained with the bulldogs and proctor waiting for them. Sooner or later they would have to go, as twelve was about to strike and they would be too late to get into their colleges. Twelve o'clock struck, with the proctor and bulldogs still waiting. The undergraduates then turned out to be Queen's College men, for they knocked at the gates and were admitted safe into their own walls.

Sometimes the proctors visit distant inns of low reputation where undergraduates are rumoured to be.

The proctors can impose a fine of up to five pounds, or they can "gate"* an undergraduate. The fine money goes to a mysterious thing called the University Chest. You may see the old University Chest, a huge iron box, on a back stair case of the Ashmolean Museum, among coins, spears, skins and arrowheads.

It is worth mentioning here that the behaviour of undergraduates in their own colleges is generally watched over by the Dean or the Junior Dean of the college. This gentleman is not often a clergyman, but a "don." In Christ Church he is called the Censor. The Dean, Junior

* This means that he cannot leave his college after Tom, the Great Bell at Christ Church, has sounded its hundred-and-one strokes at nine-ten p.m.

Radcliffe Camera.   Started 1737.
Finished 1749.   James Gibbs.

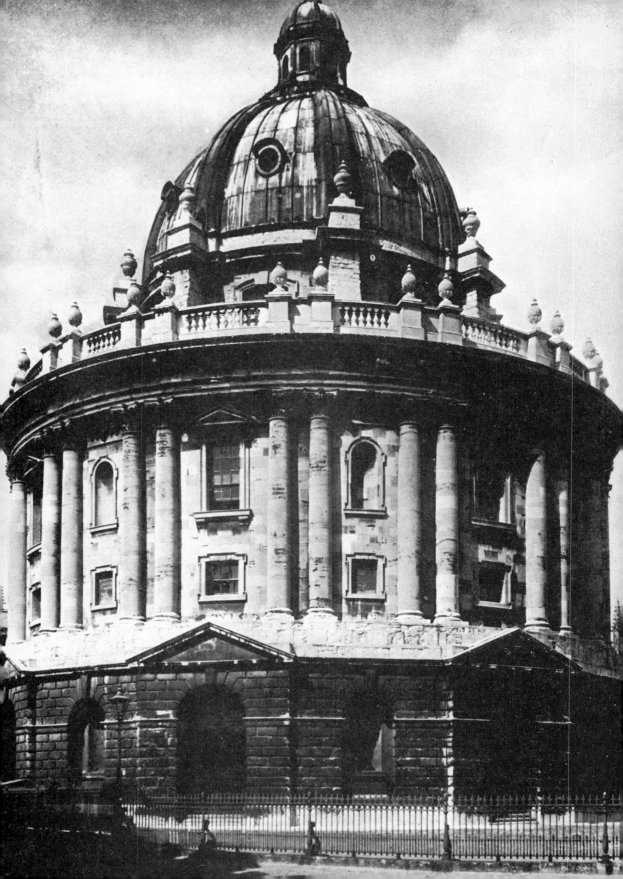

The Ashmolean Museum and Taylorian, 1841–48.

Dean or Censor acts in the college in the capacity of Adjutant where the Head of the college is the Colonel.

The proctors have other duties of a somewhat mediaeval nature, at University function. The Senior Proctor for instance can sing the exquisite Latin Litany on the first Sunday of Hilary Term in the University church, either doing it himself or by deputy.

HIGH

We are forgetting the procession.

Behind the Proctors come the HEADS OF HOUSES (Colleges) who are not doctors. They will probably be wearing the black gown and red and black hood of a Master of Arts. The head of a house has a different title. At Christ Church he is a clergyman, and called a Dean. This is because Christ Church has a Cathedral, with Canons, whose Chapter is nothing to do with the University. At other colleges the name differs. At All Souls, Keble, Merton, New College and Wadham he is called a War-den. At Balliol, Pembroke and University he is a Master. At Brasenose, Hertford, Jesus, and St. Edmund Hall, he is Principal. At Corpus Christi, Magdalen, St. John's, and Trinity, he is President.   At Exeter and Lincoln he is Rector. At Oriel, Queen's and Worcester he is Provost. Whatever he is, he is well paid, with a large house to himself and the chance of being Vice-Chancellor. The ease of the life of a Head of a House usually leads to longevity. Dr. Routh, the last President of Magdalen but two, was appointed in 1751 and lived to be an hundred. A late Provost of Queen's lived so long that pro-provosts died under him.

BROAD

Now come the MASTERS OF ARTS (M.A.), whose hoods I have already described. They are nearly all dons—

LOW

19

that is to say Professors, Lecturers, Readers or Fellows of Colleges.

They are followed by the BACHELORS OF ARTS (B.A.), who wear black hoods trimmed with rabbit fur. Hoods are a survival of monkish days, but they are no longer practical for covering the head.

Since we are nearing the end of the procession and it seems to be losing its glamour, I must speak up here for the Bachelors of Arts. Though they rank below Masters in precedence they are not necessarily less intelligent. Once you are a Bachelor you can become a Master after a short period and the payment of a fee to the University Chest. There is no examination for the honour.

Next follow a few SCHOLARS in black Russell cord gowns with yokes and short bell-shaped sleeves. These are clever young gentlemen who are still undergraduates, but have done well enough in their entrance examinations to receive money from their colleges.

Nearly last come some COMMONERS, by no means all in the University. They wear short Russell cord gowns reaching to the waist. Broad black collars turn over. There are no sleeves but two streamers decorated with squares hang down behind. These gentlemen were not clever enough to win scholarships, and so they pay for the privilege of belonging to the University.

Last of all comes the REGISTRAR who wears bands and, probably, the dress of a Master of Arts. He organized the whole thing.

The last flutter of the Registrar's gown disappearing through a stone archway, the voices of the crowd around you raised to normal pitch after the awed exclamations of admiration at so many first-class brains under such a variety of mediaeval headgear, at divers lovely robes flaring against soft-toned walls—and you will be wondering whence this pageant wound and to what old building of those that tower about you it is bound.

It came from the Vice-Chancellor's College which might have been anywhere. It is bound, under the Tower of the Five Orders whose carved gates are only opened this day in the year, for the Sheldonian Theatre that apsidal building with a little lantern on top and with those stone-bearded busts for rail posts which Americans walking down Broad Street often take for the twelve apostles.

In the Theatre an organ recital is being held to entertain the public sitting in the gallery close under the painted ceiling. Below are the empty seats ranged in the manner of an amphitheatre round the dais of the Chancellor, Vice-Chancellor and Proctors, and the reserved benches for other University members and officials.*

As the Chancellor enters, the audience rises to its feet and a march is played, followed by the National Anthem.

The various men to be honoured with degrees are signing their names in a book in the Divinity school. They are then led across to the Sheldonian. The Public Orator (of whom more later) takes them one at a time by the right hand, bows to the Chancellor and makes a little welcoming speech in Latin full of puns and quips for the initiated. The Chancellor removes his flat Tudor bonnet, makes a little speech, shakes the eminent man by the hand, puts on his cap and motions him to a seat alongside himself. When all the eminent men present have been honoured the Public Orator recites his Creweian Oration. This is like a headmaster's review of the school year at prize-giving, except that it is in Latin.

Then University prize-winners read extracts from their pieces: Stanhope Essay, Latin Prose, Gladstone Essay, Latin Verse, English Essay, Newdigate Poem. At last the Chancellor touches his cap and says: '*Dissolvimus hanc Convocationem.*

Few are sorry, for the heat and boredom have been intense to those

* *Oxford To-day.* 1915. Crosby & Aydelotte.

MEMBERS OF THE COLLEGE ARE EXPECTED TO ATTEND DIVINE SERVICE

who don't know Latin—and often to those who do. It is a reflection on the time that this ceremony is now taken seriously. Within living memory it was an occasion for enjoyment. The organist would play popular songs such as "Taa-ra-ra boom-de-ay" at the recital, the spectators in the gallery would shout out funny jokes to the eminent men and drop cherry-stones and leaflets on to the heads of the learned Doctors. Orations would be punctuated with undergraduate witticisms.

After the ceremony in the Sheldonian, the Chancellor, eminent men, Dons and officials hurry off to luncheon parties and to stately garden parties in the colleges. Then the Dons' wives appear, but the most masterful Don's wife is put out of countenance to-day by the Academic glory of her husband, striding over grass lawns in black or scarlet.

22

Part of the Old Schools Quadrangle.

Looking north from the Radcliffe Camera to the lantern of the
Sheldonian across the pinnacles of the Old Schools.

Overcome by such a cavalcade of learning, are you surprised that a woman don, with a provincial standard of values sometimes found in Oxford, said to one of the most eminent men in the country who had been given an honorary degree, and was trying to disappear from a subsequent garden-party: "But you *can't* leave before the President of Trinity!"

Chapter Two

UNDERGRADUATES

CHEERIO! BUNGHO-SKI! WE'RE 'VARSITY UNDERGRADS

There have always been sets at the University. Ephemeral publications in the University from the days of the Commonwealth to the last novel written by an undergraduate in lieu of schools, deal with the fast men, the literary men, the hearty men, and so on. We find Whitefield in the eighteenth century tentatively seeking out from Pembroke College the Methodists in Lincoln College who were led by John Wesley. Not much later there is Gibbon, making several visits to London, Buckinghamshire and Bath all in one term. He was obviously a fast man.

In the 'seventies there was Ruskin encouraging the aesthetes to rebuild the village street in North Hinksey. And there it stands to-day, commemorating the efforts of gentlemen-artist-craftsmen, among whom even Oscar Wilde was proud to push a wheelbarrow. Then there were the aesthetes of Wilde's time and Wilde's famous room at Magdalen (looking over the river behind the kitchen), with its blue china and pea-cock feathers.

It would be possible indefinitely to recount stories of various Oxford sets from the Black Magic workers in Brasenose over a hundred years

SISTERS TO TEA——1890-ISH UNDERGRADUATES

ago to their successors who were said to practise in another College shortly after the last war.

I cannot mention names nor even recount all the sets of undergraduates to be found in Oxford. But there are certain constants, certain groups which remain even to-day, particularly among the old-fashioned undergraduates, who have paid to come up.

First there are the University clubs, and these should not be confused with "sets". There are the well-known clubs, such as the O.U.D.S. for actors, the Gridiron for Old Wykehamists and their admirers, Vincent's for blues and athletic kings, and the Union for the politi-

On the roof of the Radcliffe Camera.

cally-minded and those who want tea and a nice central place for a wash-and-brush-up (it has the best lavatories of any club in Oxford), and the Labour for the Left Wing. There are the dimmer clubs of certain enthusiastic members who meet in one another's rooms. You may see notices of these clubs on the college boards opposite the porter's lodge: "The Historical Society", "The Mermaid Club", "The English Society", "The Campanology Club"—"Mr. W. Jones (Jesus) will read a paper on *The development of Bob Major into Stedman Triples in the latter half of the*

OLD-FASHIONED AESTHETES

nineteenth century'. In Mr. Williams's rooms No. 4 Staircase, Jesus College."

There are societies and clubs (some confined to a single college) connected with every pursuit of the mind. An undergraduate reading for the English school, for instance, which is really Anglo-Saxon, Northumbrian dialect and tedious mediaeval poems, will probably join a literary club to please his tutor. His tutor has probably joined because he thinks it will please his pupils just to show them that he was a boy once and can be ever such a jolly fellow when off duty. Thus an atmosphere of constraint is manufactured from the start.

What does this club do? Perhaps it reads plays but, because it is literary, plays have to be of a special period only. Probably it reads Restoration plays, particularly the bawdy ones. There is a lot of giggly talk and a lot of chuckling between the pipe-sucks as to who has got the unexpurgated edition and who has not. This is something which dons and all undergraduates have in common—"bawdiness"—good old clean,

Elizabethan and Restoration dirt. Of course you can't mention it in schools, but no harm in talking about it out of schools.

So the grey-flannelled figures squat down on the Turkey carpet and the dons lean back in their Oxford chairs; the secretary reads the minutes of the last meeting. "On Thursday, 5th November, we had an entertaining paper on 'Was Webster a dipsomaniac?' by Mr. Crapper, Fellow and Tutor of Parclose College. Mr. Crapper proved his point in a most ingenious and convincing way, citing many damning quotations from Webster's plays and from lesser known works, many of which were so lesser known as to be past the knowledge of the lesser members of the club (chuckles). A vote of thanks was passed to Mr. Crapper for providing the club with one of the most entertaining evenings it can remember. It was decided to read the *Duchess of Malfi* at the next meeting."

All the while Mr. Crapper is leaning back sucking at his pipe, while his armchair creaks as he retires further into it, out of sheer modesty. Of course Webster wasn't a dipsomaniac, but, he flattered himself, it was rather an ingenious paper and raised a laugh or two. He does not flatter himself that an undergraduate audience is more likely to laugh at a tutor's witticisms than any other. No, he goes on to think that he will work it up a bit, take out the more obvious jokes and send it up to the *Oxford University Magazine* or perhaps even the *London Mercury*. Quite a slight thing, of course, just dashed off—but scholarly, scholarly.

But what have we here! Oho! The ceremony is about to begin. Of course the club has a ceremony. A loving-cup is passed round full of mulled beer. Pipes are laid down on the floor, cigarettes flicked into the fire. The president of the club—an extraordinarily good-looking chap though not a first-rate brain—lifts the cup to his lips; in a deep voice he says the magic words:—"Genius of the Restoration—Aid our own resuscitation."—and passes it on to the next man who repeats the same rubric in solemn Liverpudlian accents (he is likely to get a first), he then drinks, leaving a slight shaving of tobacco on the silver rim. So it goes round until all have pledged themselves. The copies of the *Duchess of Malfi* are opened, unexpurgated copies so far as possible, and with parts

assigned to them, the members read while the moon shines down on the pinnacles outside.

At the end of the meeting there is a general distribution of coffee and beer—then out into the Oxford night bright with moon and the head lamps of motor-cars to guide many a well-cared-for bicycle down the Cowley Road.

Do not imagine, reader, that clubs of this sort play any part in the social life of the University. They certainly do not. Their importance is about as great as that of a Browning Society in an enlightened suburb —disseminating culture among those who have not had enough of it already.

Still the biggest non-intellectual and social influence among undergraduates is the Bullingdon Club. You will see, from Mr. Lancaster's drawing, that it consists of the well-born (and sometimes rather weedy) and the very rich. In prewar days it consisted only of the well-born. Most of its members come out of Christ Church. They wear blue and white ties. Every now and again they have a dinner. Possibly it was such a club as this which was described by Mr. Evelyn Waugh in his novel *Decline and Fall*.

BULLINGDON

"It is not accurate to call this an annual event, because quite often the Club is suspended for some years after each meeting. There is tradition behind the Bollinger: it numbers reigning kings among its past members. At the last dinner, three years ago, a fox had been brought in in a cage and stoned to death with champagne bottles. What an evening that had been! This was the first meeting since then, and from all over Europe old members had rallied for the occasion. For two days they had been pouring into Oxford: epileptic royalty from their villas of exile: uncouth peers from crumbling country seats:

After Hall.

smooth young men of uncertain tastes from embassies and legations: illiterate lairds from wet granite hovels in the Highlands: ambitious young barristers and Conservative candidates torn from the London season and the indelicate advances of debutantes; all that was most sonorous of name and title was there for the beano . . . A shriller note could now be heard rising from Sir Alastairs' rooms; any who have heard the sound will shrink at the recollection of it; it is the sound of the English county families baying for broken glass. Soon they would all be tumbling into the quad, crimson and roaring in their bottle-green evening coats, for the real romp of the evening."

Beside the Bullingdon, other clubs or societies pale. There survived until recently, and may survive still, various college dining-clubs which had peculiar, coloured evening coats in which members used to attend meetings for food and drink.

An intellectual club, too, may become a purely social affair. Some years ago there was a club which was run by the Liberal Party. It fell on bad days, and many people were elected to it whose opinions were not political and who wanted somewhere to cash a cheque and get a drink. Liberals who came into it were soon frowned on, and behaviour to them was, indeed, so marked that they left the club. The system of credit and cheques brought no more prosperity to the club, and it was eventually closed down. Lloyd George is said to have paid the debts of the club under the impression that he was helping out indigent Oxford Liberals.

The obverse of this may happen to a club. There is, let us say, a fairly successful English Society run by the women as well as men, and of course the women predominate. Whenever women come into an undergraduate club they drive the men out. This is far from their intention, but they are so desperately eager, so well-informed, so regular in attendance, and young men so much dislike being snubbed or argued with by women students, that unless they are in love they cease their mem-

From the opposite bank to the college barges, and he will allow no bad language in his boat.

Encouragement.

bership. Let us go on with this suppositious English Club. The women who have now got the upper hand take their opinions from their tutors. The tutors take their opinions from *The Times Literary Supplement*, *The Spectator*, *The Review of English Studies*, and The Book Society. Well-known middle-brow authors are asked down to speak.

Then the intellectuals rebel, the surrealists, the left-wingers, the right-wingers, the social climbers, the buyers of quadrimestials. They are scandalized and form the New English Club, to which some young poet is asked whose works have so far only appeared in a short-lived paper published in Paris. He electrifies the young men, joyful in their rebellion. But Heaven protect them if they mention what they have heard in schools. No rot like that there. And the offended members of the old English Club, some of whom are dons, will remember the young rebels when examination papers are to be corrected.

Diversions like these in all branches of art, learning, and even sport, occupy the conversation of those undergraduates in the know and they are, almost without exception, those who pay to come up and a few college scholars.

We are gradually emerging from the mixture of clubs and societies, into the less definable realms of undergraduate sets. Many of the more unenterprising young men never get any further outside their dull round of working for schools than some little club, where any needs of their souls, other than answering questions which *may* be set by the examiners, are amply provided for. The hardest-working political economist may like an hour off a week to discuss bell-ringing. In the campanology club, he dares to stand himself a drink and expand.

But the social undergraduate goes farther than a club. He finds himself in a set, among friends who have common sympathies. The more usual sympathies—sport, beer, or communism—he may find in his own college. And if he is one of those simple fellows, he will remain a college man. The fact that he has to leave his rooms in the college for his last year or two years and take others in lodgings in the town, while still

SPORTIN' MEN

remaining a member of the college, will not prevent his returning to the beloved place every day. He will haunt the porter's lodge, turn up regularly in hall, shout abusively at people he doesn't like, be very friendly with people he hopes will like him, talk loudly and in a proprietary manner when any visitors to the college are walking about admiring its architecture, join all the college clubs, have nicknames for the dons and treat the

place as his dear old schooldays all over again with beer and a little more bawdiness thrown in.

Besides the sporting type of college man, there is the "college spirit" man. He has generally been inculcated with principles of loyalty at his public school. He does not like to give them up. Of course the college isn't quite the same as the dear old school, because he isn't there quite so long. He may not be good at games. In that case he joins in with all sets. The ones he most admires are the beer and sport fellows. Toadying to athletes comes naturally to all people who have been educated at almost any school; it is a tradition with them. But now he is grown up a bit; he will take an interest in art too and, by Jove! literature. So one day he calls on the leading literary man, who doesn't have much to do with the college because he is so frightfully stand-offish, and says: "I say, do tell me something about books." And the leading literary man, flattered, perhaps attracted by him or perhaps sorry for him, shows him a copy of *The New Criterion*. So the college spirit man buys a copy of *The New Criterion* and perhaps the poems of Gerard Manley Hopkins, and he puts them beside his J. B. Priestley and his Examination Statutes, and the A. P. Herbert book he got as a leaving prize, all on the little hanging bookshelf in his room, with its tobacco jar with the college crest, its photographs of mum and dad with college crests on the frames and its "Oxford" chair. And those are the only little books of culture he will ever see. And when many years later, he sits with his wife in their snug little home at Wokingham, he will point with his pipe stem at *The New Criterion* and the Hopkins and say: "Yes, I was interested in Hopkins and that sort of thing once—" and his little wife will be ever so proud of his knowing about something she doesn't understand.

But he never understood it, either. There comes a time when that literary man becomes unpopular. The athletic toughs decide to cut his hair and raid his rooms and smash his piano and burn his books. Then our "college spirit" man can come into his own. Then he can say: "The fellow is just a poseur—why, art is only filth— pornography—bestiality—sodomy—and Hopkins—why, no one understands him. Old Snooks (the nickname of the English don) says he's not a poet at all—just rubbish!" So Tallyho! he surges up the stairs with the others, and helps to break up the piano and to tear up the books —a prominent man for the one and only time in his life.

The status of these college sets varies with the status of the college. For many years now, Christ Church, judged by Debrett standards, has stood highest. It was followed by Magdalen, with New College third. Magdalen has sunk in the last few years in the Debrett category. Trinity has a very high percentage of men from the larger public schools. New College, by reason of its foundation statutes, is primarily Wykhamical. "*Educ.:* Winchester and New College, Oxford" appears in "Who's Who" after the name of many a knighted civil servant and successful barrister. And if few New College men are distinguished or even lovable characters, there is no doubt that they run the country less obtrusively but more certainly than those Christ Church peers who once drank themselves silly at Bullingdon dinners.

Other colleges rise and sink, though some retain characteristics, sometimes connected with their foundations. Exeter is West Country and High Church. Wadham was West Country and Evangelical. Balliol is Scottish and intellectual. Indeed Balliol produces more distinguished men, in politics and literature, than any other college. Its famous run of scholars in the nineteenth century causes one to look at its hideous Broad Street façade with superstitious awe. Brasenose is tough and athletic; indeed, there is even said to be a scholarship for Rugby Football at this college. Oriel is connected with Rhodes, and therefore Colonial. Queen's has very good food. Pembroke has a good cellar. Worcester and St. John's have nice gardens. Jesus is full of Welshmen.

Merton is gay and hospitable. Corpus is hardworking. Lincoln University, St. Edmund Hall, Hertford and Keble are less definable. All Souls does not count, as it only consists of dons.

One college set, however, remains the same, whatever the status of the college. This consists of the dim men. It can hardly be called a set,

UNION

because few of the dim men know each other. They creep out of their rooms to the hall and speak to nobody. Their rooms are a blank. The college furniture is there—the cumbrous sofa, the carpet with holes in it, the table with its baize cover, the looking-glass over the chimney-piece, a packet of ten Players and one of those enormous boxes of "Club" matches, the only extravagance of many a college stores, a few unreadable books from the library, entirely connected with schools, and some left wing politics in cheap editions, an uninjured cap and gown—and its occupant as neutral as the walls.

Next year the dim man will go to lodgings down some distant suburban road in Oxford which looks exactly like somewhere in Luton. He will pursue his silent way. Back to college to see if there is any new rule to obey; regular attendance at all lectures : a short walk in the afternoon : a long read in the Library until ten o'clock, and back in complete silence to the suburban street. What pains, what cocoa, what eyestrain will have gone to get him his second! What an unaccountable form of slavery Oxford will seem, if ever, years afterwards, he gets a sense of perspective!

So much for the college sets and the colleges. But there is considerable inter-college life from the Bullingdon upwards (or downwards, however you care to look at it). It would be interesting to trace how the influences on a decade are reflected in the important branches of inter-collegiate life.

In the earlier part of the nineteenth century the Oxford Movement brought people together from all colleges. In the later part, scholarship and social life. North Oxford parties and clever people down from London are the talk of many books of the late nineteenth century reminiscences. Mrs. Mark Pattison made gracious flitting visits to her husband's functions.

In the nineteen-twenties when there was little for men to put faith in, sex-talk was a bond. Now it is politics with communism in the ascendant. There is no doubt that the strongest inter-collegiate bonds among undergraduates to-day are similar political sympathies. Communism in the University has done much to make Oxford comprehensible to the state-subsidized man—or incomprehensible for its inconsistency.

It is significant that college dances at the end of the Summer term, which were all crowded out in pre-war and even post-war days, have now become almost failures. There is not the money to keep them up, for one thing, since the poor are in the majority; there is not the inclination to go, for another. Undergraduates are off to Labour camps and workers' tours of Soviet Russia.

GAMES

Apart from the political sets, which are the biggest and most truly democratic undergraduate groups with a higher percentage of state-subsidized men than any others, there are the other inter-collegiate sets which have existed for years.

The rich men who are not in the Bullingdon but who would like to be, and the Bullingdon men, lead a life on their own. They wear checks. They wear whole suits, well cut. They frequently get leave to go up to London. They drive away every day to fashionable eating-places, races and country houses in cars. They rarely bother about examinations. They are more often seen in a hat than in cap and gown.

The athletic kings are another intercollege set not to be confused with the toughs who form the college sport and beer sets. The really grand athletes sit about in Vincent's, are looked up to by the dons, and may be acquainted with some of the rich men. To the literary and political world, they are unknown.

A large intercollege set is that connected with literature and the arts.

37

It contains more impostors than any other set, but it also contains the best jokes and the best conversation. It is impossible to specify what forms of literature and art is popular with this set. One may safely assume one that has not yet penetrated to the majority of the dons, few of whom have any visual sense.

Ten years ago a reproduction of Van Gogh's sunflowers and Eliot's poems might be found in every aesthete's rooms. Now Van Gogh remains, and Auden and Day Lewis have given place to the Sitwells and Mr. Eliot. The artistic and literary gentleman is expected to take an interest in music. He generally has a gramophone and some Bach records, some of the more subtle dance records, and never Wagner. This is sometimes described as aesthetic, and until lately "aesthetes" were easily recognizable for their long hair or odd clothes. With the advent of left-wing politics into modern verse, the aesthete has slightly changed his appearance. He is a little scrubby-looking nowadays; his tie alone flames out. Where in old days he was keen on food and affected an interest in wine, he is now more keen about a good hike or bicycle ride with a friend or a long draught of beer among the workers. It is unsafe to generalize too boldly about the aesthetes. They retain an individuality more, perhaps, than any other collection of undergraduates.

A further intercollege set is the acting one, members of the Oxford University Dramatic Society or other amateur players. Here the small talk of green-room life is learnt with rapidity, "props," "drying-up," and the various stage terms for Shakespeare's plays: *The Dream, Dicky Three Strokes* (Richard III), *Lear*, etc. The actors link up with the aesthetes just so much as actors link up with literary men in the outer world. That is to say, some actors are minor literary men, and lesser aesthetes are pleased to be connected with them.

Religion certainly makes intercollege sets, but with these undergraduates the focal point is not a club nor a dinner, but some place of worship, varying in the Church of England from High Mass at Pusey House to Holy Supper in the Evening at Holy Trinity, Gas Street. It is a mistake to imagine that the religious undergraduates are necessarily reading theology for a degree. The more promising ones are not.

O.U.D.S.

There is one more set yet, the "fast" set. And by the use of the word "fast," I intend no moral censure in the way of a Victorian novel. The "fast" men are great dancers. They meet for coffee at eleven o'clock at varying fashionable centres. They hang about the more attractive undergraduettes. Their rooms are full of broken gramophone records, cigarette ends and empty bottles. The springs of their sofas are gone. They have great fun voting for *La Vie Parisienne* to be subscribed for in Junior Common Room. They are more like stockbrokers than you would believe possible in an Oxford man. There is something a little squalid about them when compared with the rich and snobbish sets. Their affairs are a little coarse—any girl who can be got and a mock love-affair after too much luncheon. Many of these poor fellows have spots on their faces and wear check caps.

I suppose it is only right to bring in undergraduettes, but in bringing them in, it would be wrong to give an impression that they play a large part in the social life of the University. They vary among themselves, no doubt, as much as the men. You may see nuns at lectures, you may also see women, in gay dresses under their caps and gowns, who have obviously attended to be admired. Now and then you will meet some outstanding character, attractive and intelligent. Her influence will pervade a large part of the University. She will keep her virtue and her popularity. She will fire many young men with a respect for women, by the gracious contrast she makes with the female brain-boxes and some of the women-dons. For the majority of women students are embryo school-mistresses who take everything literally, make copious notes at lectures, talk to one another about the lecturer afterwards, do not bother about their personal appearances, carry

A SOUND SECOND

hundreds of books in the little wicker baskets in front of the handle-bars of their bicycles. They think about examinations, and any who think about other things are unlikely to earn the approval of dons.

There are tales of the wild life in women's colleges, of "cocoa crushes", and of a woman-don who was so much worshipped that undergraduettes slept on the carpet outside her door, until the don was asked to resign. But there is no means of finding out whether such stories are true.

What is certain, is that women do drive out many good men from the clubs and the societies they invade. They, too, are partly responsible for the raising of the standard of examinations, because they work so much more doggedly than many of the men. The men are not attracted by "brilliant" women, they are only grateful if they are pretty.

The subject of higher education for women is out of place in this book. But women are vastly handicapped in getting the full value of

Blackwell's Bookshop; to many an excellent free library of books in "mint" condition (*above*).
A Broad Street stationery shop, now destroyed, for the Bodleian extension (*below*).

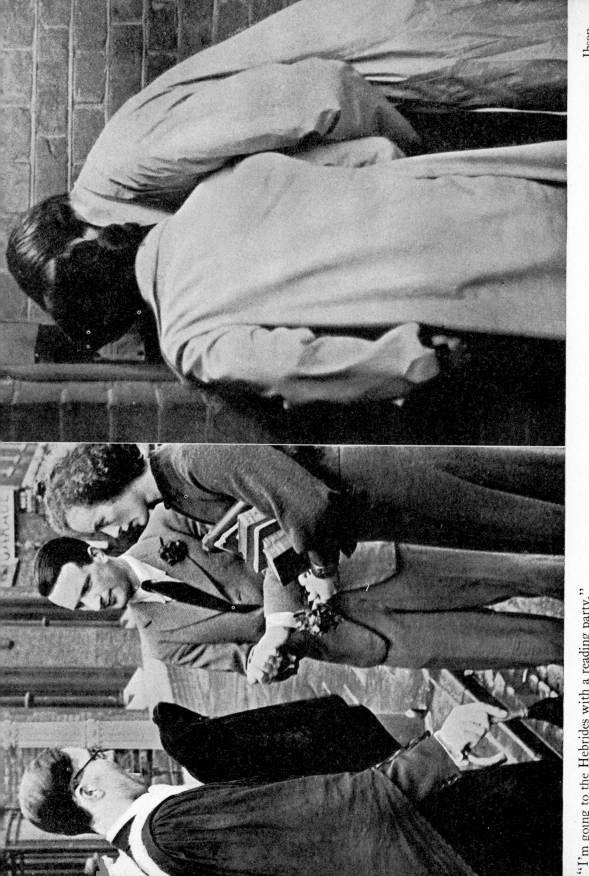

Ibsen.

"I'm going to the Hebrides with a reading party."

Oxford life. They live too far away, they think too much about "work," they are the wrong sex for free-and-easy conversation among clever but gauche schoolboys.

The subject of sex at Oxford is greatly discussed in the outside world and in Oxford itself. Indeed, except for politics, it is about the most popular subject, even more popular than dialectical materialism. Homosexuality goes in waves, just as it does in public schools. One college may be notorious for it one year, and another the next. It is talked about far more than it is practised. Though it would be difficult for any undergraduate, however dim, to avoid a discussion sometime or other in his career, on homosexuality, it would be an error to imagine that every undergraduate is likely to start practising it as a result of such discussion. Far more likely he will learn tolerance of a failing which is not his own and buy a pocket A.B.C. of psycho-analysis.

Certain of the less athletic sets contain homosexuals who have great and famous love-affairs. Such affairs are not by

A BRAIN-REFRESHING TRAMP TO SHOTOVER

any means entirely physical, but mixed up with friendship, Edward Carpenter, John Addington Symonds, Plato and long walking tours. The athletic and tougher sets may let themselves go after a long period of such training; their behaviour can scarcely be called homosexuality, but is rather an extension of furtive affairs in the changing room at school and can be put down to nothing more complicated than the absence of women.

41

In no set is there a very much higher percentage of genuine homo sexuals than there is in any other society. Someone who has " tenden-cies" as an undergraduate, will in ten years time be settled down to married life.

State-subsidized undergraduates are generally heterosexual. Prob-ably they may have a fine romance with an undergraduette and will marry when they go down. In that case the undergraduette has per-formed a better service than getting her usual second after three years unremitting work.

AN INDUSTRIAL WORKER AT OXFORD

By

Ernest J. Marsh

Before coming up to Oxford with an Extra-Mural Scholarship I had, in common with a number of other industrial workers, been attending a tutorial class run under the Oxford University Tutorial Classes Com-mittee. Many undergraduates find it difficult to realize that large numbers of working men and women are pursuing, so far as their limited leisure time will allow, much the same kind of studies as themselves. Indeed whatever criticisms may be made against Oxford one of the great things which stands to its credit is that it has, in the

THE FRESHMAN'S DREAM

TYPICAL BEDROOM 1830 OR 1930

important part which it has played in the development of the adult education movement, helped to bring the University to the workers in response to a demand which sprang from the workers themselves.

As do most elementary schoolboys, at the age of fourteen I handed in my school books for the last time. The school adjoined the local railway works and, such was the rapidly maturing effect of passing to the factory side of the playground wall, many of us who were schoolboys one day became railwaymen the next. We were inordinately proud of our black faces and grimy clothes. Indeed the grimier we were the greater we considered our superiority over our former schoolfellows. I soon discovered however, as I've no doubt my companions did also, that the gulf between myself and my schooldays was infinitely wider than the thickness of the playground wall.

At sixteen, when most boys are apprenticed to one of the trades in which there happens to be a vacancy, my desire to become a skilled craftsman was frustrated. Work in the railway industry was slack. Finally, after working as a rivet lad with a gang of riveters, I was allotted a semi-skilled job in the boiler shop. For several years I worked at a forge with a smith whose good nature I shall always remember with affection, and whose craftsmanship I shall always admire.

It is unnecessary for any man to have spent some years doing a monotonous routine job in a factory in order to appreciate either the beauty of Oxford or the opportunity which it provides him of devoting the greater part of his time to those studies in which his real interest lies. The contrast in environment however between the drab whitewashed walls of the workshop with its deafening tattoo of riveting hammers, and the noble buildings and cloistered quiet of the University, has perhaps made me value certain features of life in Oxford more than the undergraduate who has come straight up from either a public or secondary school. The complete absence of the heat and noise of the factory has been a refreshing change.

Instead of getting up between six-thirty and seven I now get up at eight. After a more leisurely meal than when breakfast had to be swallowed hastily with one eye on the clock, I settle down to read. There is just time for two and a half hours' work, reading and taking notes in preparation for my weekly essay, before attending a lecture in the Examination Schools at eleven. Whether attendance at lectures be regarded as work or recreation depends largely upon the lecturer. At all events I usually come away with fewer notes for future reference from those lectures which have been most enjoyable and stimulating. Since heckling is not permitted I have not yet heard an undergraduate admonish a lecturer to "speak up" though I have sometimes felt an urge to do so. Perhaps the fault lies in the fact that there is no charge for admission. Undergraduates, I find, are much more articulate in places where there is a box office at the entrance.

OXFORD BREAKFAST

I allow myself ten minutes to get to the Schools. I have become accustomed to taking my gown, and no longer, as happened several times at first, have to dash back and fetch it. Moreover the discovery that academic dress in Oxford attracts no more attention than blue overalls in an industrial town soon rids one of any feeling of self consciousness. That I was not, at the outset, alone in this respect, I found when a friend who had been a miner called on me in my rooms the day we were matriculated with his mortar board in a brown paper bag. After a short time I was informed that the drab garment which I at first regarded as a somewhat useless relic of mediaevalism had, unlike most vestigial remains, certain practical advantages. and served admirably the purpose of drawing up fires and keeping out draughts.

As I hurry down the High I pass three young men, ill-clad and with pinched faces, trailing despondently in the gutter bearing sandwich boards. They make a vivid contrast to the groups of well-dressed and healthy looking students hurrying past them. I recollect having read that on one occasion as John Ruskin was about to enter the Ashmolean to deliver a lecture on art in Oxford, he noticed a little girl outside whipping a top, the chastisement of which was impeded by a pair of battered shoes several sizes too large for her. He said that he felt that their concern was not with art in Oxford now, but "Why do our little girls wear large shoes?"

It is impossible for me, sitting in the warmth and comfort of the Examination Schools, not to feel that it is a part of my concern why three youths, members of my own class, should be compelled to submit to the indignity of slouching in the gutter flaunting above their heads advertisements for wares which they, and thousands like them, sorely need but cannot buy. I am reminded too, that at the last inter-college debate I attended, one of the undergraduate speakers prefaced his remarks by saying that it was extremely difficult for him to speak on the subject, which was the Means Test, as his father made him a personal allowance of five pounds a week. Such an income, I am compelled to reflect, would be affluence to many of my former workmates who have to support a wife and family on two pounds a week less than that.

Oxford, it is true, can no longer be regarded as the playground of the idle rich, yet in no other place that I have been in have I observed so clearly the anomalies in our social and educational systems.

However, the lecturer appears. It is time to pay attention to other things. The talk that has been going on ceases abruptly, with the exception of a small group of undergraduettes who remain oblivious of everything but the topic which they are discussing with considerable animation. At lectures the women usually appear to be better acquainted with each other than the men.

COLLEGE CHAPEL

The lecturer pauses hopefully, but without the desired result. He coughs apologetically, as though reluctant to interrupt. A dead silence follows.

He is in good form this morning, and makes a gallant effort to infuse life into his subject. Only a few of his witticisms at the expense of previous commentators on the text with which he is dealing fall flat. He talks steadily for an hour accompanied by the furious scratching of pens. At twelve o'clock he ceases as abruptly as he had begun, and sweeps out of the room with such rapidity that he appears to be uttering his last words as he disappears through the doorway.

I decide to spend the remaining hour before lunch in the English room at the Bodleian. Here one has the great advantage of being able to choose one's own books from the shelves. I take down a volume of Dr. Johnson's *Lives of the Poets* and continue to read until Big Tom chimes the hour. I push my book aside and go across to the college stores for lunch; as I've no doubt the author of the book I have been reading would often liked to have done when he felt hungry.

A glass of milk and a couple of sandwiches are sufficient as I am dining in hall in the evening. The college stores is a popular institution and, as usual, is crowded. In one corner a group of rowing men are discussing their chances in "Toggers." Beside me, as I munch my sandwiches, an earnest looking youth with an American accent is explaining to another group, President Roosevelt's election policy.

After lunch I call on a friend in Queen's who, like myself, has been a railwayman. Though I previously took an active interest in athletic sport, I have found walking the most pleasant form of exercise. Indeed exercise of some sort is imperative if one is to keep fit in the sluggish atmosphere of Oxford.

HEDONIST AND AVERAGE MAN

We set off along the banks of the Isis and branch off towards Cumnor Hill. We climb steadily the hill and, like Mathew Arnold's Scholar Gypsy

"Turn once to watch, while thick the snowflakes fall,
The line of festal light in Christ-Church hall—."

Here we pause to gaze down into the hollow in which the glistening spires of the colleges lie spread before us. The excessively ugly structure of the gasworks protrudes in the foreground, an unseemly reminder of the modern world's encroachment upon the ancient city of learning. The aristocratic elegance of Magdalen stands out clearly beyond the reverend antiquity of Tom Tower, but though we strain our eyes Balliol, with becoming reticence, remains indistinguishable from the rest of the city.

An hour or so later over honeyed toast and tea in Queens we discuss politics, books, and people. With a room of his own a man can, in Dr. Johnson's phrase, "Stretch his legs and have his talk out." Oxford is sometimes maligned as being a place where young men do little but talk. There is however something to be gained from exchanging views with men whose experience of life has been entirely different from one's own. Nor is it claiming too much to say that the necessity of meeting with reasoned argument the other fellow's point of view does, in the atmosphere which prevails in an Oxford college, help to create that spirit of tolerance which is indispensable to the growth of democracy.

Finally we conclude that if either of us is to get any work done before dinner the discussion, which has taken a wayward course from the Italo-Abyssinian dispute to the novels of Thomas Hardy, must be adjourned. I leave my friend to struggle with the philosophy of Kant and return to my rooms where I spend two hours on an old English translation before going into hall.

After dinner, Robson, a likeable youngster with whom I have been friendly since the Freshman's dinner, suggests coffee in the Junior Common Room. The secretary of the College Debating Society approaches and tries to persuade us to attend the debate he has arranged for that evening.

"What's the subject?" I ask.

"That there is more importance attached to getting a Blue than a First," he replies, and then volunteers the further information, as though it were a special inducement to attend, that the visitors are from one of the women's colleges.

Alpha, Beta and Gamma talking across the road after Schools.
Notice the white bow tie worn for Examinations.

"No undergraduate may be out after midnight without special leave."
A way of rendering the gates of Trinity College impregnable
to those who would scale them.

I explain that I have an essay to finish for a tutorial at ten the next morning. Besides, not only have I just refused Robson's invitation to go to a show at the Playhouse, but it is the beginning of the week, and I am still addicted to the proletarian habit of seeking my entertainment on Saturday evenings.

Robson wanders off to try and impress upon someone else the importance of the drama as a part of a liberal education, and after a glance at the evening paper I go back to my rooms to finish the essay which I have to read to my tutor in the morning.

Before coming up to Oxford I had heard a lecturer refer to someone as being as unapproachable as an Oxford don. I experienced some apprehension at the thought of having to produce a weekly essay for an unbending pedant whose relationship with me would be strictly academic and impersonal. I soon discovered however that dons, at least those with whom I had any contact, were not only quite human, but very friendly, and that passing through the College porch was not like taking up one's ticket at the factory gate. No undergraduate is made to feel that he is merely a cog in a vast machine. He retains his own individuality, and is treated as an individual. His work is judged by the amount and quality of himself that he expresses in it. The result is that the youth of twenty at the University has a more fully developed personality than his counterpart who is engaged in the mass production methods of modern industry.

The personal contact between

FIRST STEPS IN DRINKING

tutor and undergraduate which the tutorial system provides is undoubtedly of great value. That Oxford merely continues the individual educational methods to which the majority of undergraduates have already been accustomed is shown by the fact that in the public schools there are twelve boys to one master; in the secondary schools one teacher to every twenty-two pupils; while in the elementary schools there is still overcrowding to the extent of more than six thousand classes with more than fifty in each class.

On several occasions while home on vacation I have been asked how I get on with the public school men. As individuals I found them rather reserved at first but extremely friendly as soon as I got to know them. Nevertheless from the talks I have had with those who are up from the well-known public schools I have become convinced that the existence of such schools under our present educational system creates a gulf in society which only a few rare spirits with the broad and sympathetic outlook of men like R. H. Tawney and Dr. Temple are able to bridge. The environment and training of the average public schoolboy are so widely different from that of the boy who leaves an elementary school and enters industry at fourteen, that the two seldom come within hailing distance of each other. Oxford has, in fact, merely strengthened my feeling that if the public schools are, as one is led to believe, an asset to the nation, and that their teaching inculcates a true regard for things that are worth while, then there is every reason for a more democratic diffusion of their inheritance.

BRIBING A PEELER

Oxford does not, with all that it has to offer, lull the memory into forgetfulness of faces seen in the glare of a factory furnace. But one would scarcely be human to live within its precincts for a while without feeling deeply its magic charm. It does, among other things, give one a respect for learning and the discipline it requires, and makes one realize the value of education not only as a means for the development of individual character and capacity, but as an equipment for the exercise of social rights and responsibilities.

DRUNK, NOT DEAD

Chapter Three

DONS

"Is it from here the people come,
Who talk so loud, and roll their eyes,
And stammer? How extremely rum!
How curious! What a great surprise."
—H. BELLOC. *Dedicatory Ode.*

"It has been calculated that on an average an Oxford man lives for thirty-three years after taking his B.A."—Henry Robinson, D.D. (St. Albans Hall, 1838) in *London Society*, 1887.

I

Dons are senior members of the University—graduates as opposed to undergraduates—who reside at the college or somewhere in Oxford and who are engaged either in researching into their own subjects or else teaching undergraduates, or, in some cases, combining both functions. Dons have been more attacked than almost any other class of men. Before going into their characters, I must point out the opinions they hold of one another. This will help to explain the unpopularity of what seems on first glance, to be an unbalanced, strife-

Y.ᵉ MASTER OF BELLYOL

FW

ridden community. I do not mean the personal opinions dons have of one another—a don's hatred of another is a yellow, crafty thing that lasts a lifetime nor spares the memory of the dead. There is a don who so dislikes his colleagues that he takes in the novels of Berta Buck to read when obliged to sit next to his companions at meals at high table. Thus deeply can a don despise the rest on personal grounds.

The opinions I wish to give are those of a don regarding the duties of other dons.

There are the research dons. They say that the object of a University is to further learning.* The Professor and his assistants in research, must be the best men at their subjects. Only by being in the forefront of contemporary thought on their subjects, can they hope to inspire those under them with a desire to learn. A university, they say, is a home for first-class brains, not a place where people are to throw away their ability on students who are either unwilling or unable to appreciate the gems of learning presented to them. Some great brains, they say, should never be allowed the hampering necessity of meeting and teaching undergraduates at all. These great brains should be left to conduct their researches among ancient manuscripts or glass retorts.

Here, of course, comes a division among the research dons. The mathematical or science professor will say that it is infinitely more important to discover something about time or poison gas or the internal combustion engine than about the Greek particles. The classical don

* By learning they mean specialization.

will say that the right understanding of a Greek particle is a greater boon than time, poison gas, or the motor car. The history don will prefer a discovery about the open field system, the philologist about Northumbrian dialect, the economist about a law of demand and so on.

A rich man will be introduced to a high table and if it is thought that he may endow a chair of something, or a Research Fellowship of a few hundred a year to the college, the scramble, the plotting and the backbiting flourish.

On only one matter are the Research enthusiasts agreed and that is on the uselessness of the dons who confine their activities to teaching. They describe them as mere hacks. How can they, they say, know anything about their subject, while they are spending the whole time cramming people for examinations? How can they fire their pupils with enthusiasm, when they do not give themselves the time to keep in touch with the latest advances in the subject which they teach? And from this argument follows the one that teaching dons are inferior brains, who are not clever enough to do research and who deaden the enthusiasm of pupils who might otherwise be quite promising.

The teaching dons have equally weighty arguments against research. Specialization, they say, is all very well in medical and scientific departments, but in other schools, such as modern languages it is out of place. Specialization for instance, has turned a school mis-called English Literature into a collection of the texts of mediaeval allegoric poets and the study of mutations in Anglo-Saxon. Nothing is too remote for the specialist. If his subject is not abstruse enough—if it has in it an element of aesthetic appreciation such as one would suppose to exist in the school of English Literature—then it must be turned into a science.* It is the attitude of the late Sir Walter Raleigh, protagonist of literature, against Professor Wyld, protagonist of research into philology. With the death

*See *Eng: Lit:* by Stephen Potter. Cape.

of Sir Walter Raleigh, most people conclude that the study of English literature at Oxford, died too.

The research virus, say the teaching dons, infects a man who is slightly priggish and turns him into a pedant while he is still in his early twenties. This embryo specialist is described by G. A. K. in *Oxford—A Last Phase** as "no dilettante. He is the professional scholar. He is the specialist, the expert, and nothing more. His subject is all that matters to him. He must devote all his time and all his energies to the furthering of it. And from his pupils he will expect the same devotion. They will meet with approval in his eyes in proportion as they give indications of being themselves potential furtherers. How his particular subject fits in with other subjects, and if there is a right perspective to view his subject in, are questions that do not arise."

Teaching dons, therefore, stress the importance of inspired teaching, but they do not think that the research man who is top of his subject, is necessarily an inspired teacher.

Research and teaching dons can sometimes find themselves in agreement on the subject of women dons. Many male dons dislike women dons, and it is certainly rare to find a woman don who is welcomed in either professional or tutorial circles. The dislike may be engendered by personal jealousy between the sexes. There still prevails an opinion among men that women are better minding their distaffs than correcting Greek accents. A pretty undergraduette can be excused: but a pretty woman don seems an anomaly. Few male dons will put up the anti-feminist argument, as it is too obvious and lays them open to attack. They say, instead, that women alter the standards of examination. They over-emphasize the necessity for reading and learning and sitting up night after night intoxicated by the fumes of bad coffee, learning lists and arguments and references. The stricter discipline of a woman's

* *The National Review.* February, 1934.

56

Dr. Frewen in the Bodleian.

"Verify your references." The Bodleian.

college, makes it possible for women to get in more work. Women dons, say the anti-feminists, discountenance genius at the expense of hard work. It is possibly true that women get more indifferent firsts and sound seconds in the schools, than startling firsts or glorious thirds. Those men who have been examined *viva voce* by a woman don will remember the searching questions into printed facts, the negation of any chance of covering up the lack of knowledge with abundance of wits.

"ARE YOU SURE SHE HAS AN ALPHA MIND?"

The women dons retaliate on the men by extreme punctiliousness in matters of university procedure. They are intensely accurate. They know their stuff—and it is a great thing to floor a male don in his own subject. They are well up in University jargon. Phrases "first-class brains" "essentially gamma-minded" "sub-fusc" and "the Giler" are continually on their lips.

Whether there should be women dons or whether women should be allowed a university training at all, is a question too large for the scope of this book. It is a matter of the equality of the sexes and one on which it seems to me, only a hermaphrodite can give an impartial judgment.

II

Into such a world of plot and counterplot, through which only a celestial being could pass undisturbed, is the young don let loose. So far we have considered dons in a purely professional light. Now comes the human element and here the plot and counterplot becomes more complicated still.

Dons are only human, we are told, though the statement wants qualification. It needs a firm spirit indeed to withstand the organization—if the conflicts there described can be called organization—of University life. Creature comfort tempts on one side, ambition on another, pedantry on a third.

There was a time when dons were notorious for human failings:

"It is a notorious truth that most candidates get leave of the proctor, by paying his man a crown (which is called his perquisite), to choose their own examiners, who never fail to be their old cronies and toping companions."—*Terrae Filius. June* 8, 1720–1. "The fellows or monks of my time were decent easy men who supinely enjoyed the gifts of their Founder. From the toil of reading, or thinking or writing, they had absolved their conscience."—*Edward Gibbon* (Magdalen; matriculated 1752). *Miscellaneous works. Vol. I, London* 1796. "My tutor, an excellent and worthy man, according to the practice of all tutors at that moment, gave himself no concern about his pupils. I never saw him but during a fortnight, when I took it into my head to be taught trigonometry."—*James Harris, First Earl of Malmesbury* (Merton; matriculated 1763) *Diaries and Correspondence* 1844. *Vol. I.*

" . . . . for it is reckoned good management to get acquainted with two or three jolly young masters of arts, and supply them well with port, previously to the examinations. . . . As neither the officer [Vice-Chancellor and proctors], nor anyone else, usually enters the room (for it is reckoned very ungenteel) the examiners and the candidates often converse on the last drinking-bout, or on horses, or read the newspaper, or a novel or divert themselves as well as they can in any manner, till the clock strikes eleven, when all parties descend, and the *testimonium* is signed by the masters."—*Vicesimus Knox* (St. Johns Matr: 1771). *Essays Moral and Literary. Vol. I.* 1782. " 'Am I to understand, sir, that you adopt the principles contained in this work?' or some such words; for like one red with the suffusion of college port and college ale, the intense heat of anger seemed to deprive him of the power of articulation; by reason of a rude provincial dialect, and thickness of utterance, his speech being at all times indistinct. 'The last question is still more improper than the former.' I replied—for I felt that the imputation was an insult; 'and since, by your own act, you have renounced all authority over me, our communication is at an end.' 'I command you to quit my college to-morrow at an early hour.' I bowed and withdrew. I thank God I have never seen that man since: he is gone to his bed, and there let him sleep. Whilst he lived, he ate freely of the scholar's bread, and drank from his cup; and he was sustained, throughout the whole term of his existence, wholly and most nobly, by those sacred funds that were consecrated by our pious forefathers to the advancement of learning."—*P. B. Shelley's account of his expulsion from University College* 1811 *for publishing a pamphlet on the Necessity of Atheism. From T. J. Hogg's Life of P. B. Shelley* 1858.

I regard Shelley's outburst as symptomatic of the phase in University life which was to turn Oxford from a place where sons of noble families went to learn to hold their liquor and ripen friendships, a place where dons were people of little account and learned gentlemen amiable eccentrics, to a place designed for work only. I think Shelley would hardly have been in sympathy with such a gentleman as Dr. T. E. Kebbel, had he lived to see him. Mr. Kebbel was at Oxford in the late 'forties and the Oxford he knew then must have been little different from the Oxford of Shelley's day. By 1876 when Mr. Kebbel had grown into a High Church barrister, Oxford had been subjected to the first of its constitutional reforms which helped to turn it from a University to a Polytechnic and, indeed a place, theoretically at any rate, suited to Shelley. In that year Mr. Kebbel let himself go in the *Cornhill Magazine*.

"The life of undergraduates has changed as well as their attire. The introduction into the University of quite a new class of men, belonging to the lower rank of life has led to the formation of new social habits among men of the old stamp, which are, however, but an inadequate compensation for what has passed away. In the pre-Reform days, the whole body of Oxford men were, in many respects like one gigantic common room: all members of a highly exclusive society; all members of the Church, and, with some very few exceptions who did not in the slightest degree affect the tone or manners of the place, all gentlemen. . .

"Lastly, there is the alteration in the status of the Fellows themselves. A don in my day was only partially associated in the undergraduate mind with the ideas of education and learning. Each college was then a close, powerful, and wealthy corporation, doing what it liked with its own, repelling interference from without, and, perhaps it is hardly too much to say, a little University in itself. . . . In Oxford and Cambridge alone were found these ancient immemorial nests of life-long leisure, the occupants of which succeeded each other like rooks in a rookery, when the tall elms tell of centuries of undisturbed repose and inviolate prescription.   Individual birds were very often laughed at, it is true; but collectively they shared in the respect which was paid to the system as a whole; and helped to invest the idea of 'Donship' in general with attributes very different from the admiration and sympathy which we feel for every clever set of schoolmasters, lecturers, and professors."

Mr. Kebbel was aware of the change in social conditions of the outside world and his lament is merely a lament, not a stricture. But if he could have written like that in the late Victorian era, how much more would he have lamented had he lived to see the Oxford of to-day. The Oxford of the 'seventies was still an Oxford where cultivated eccentrics and various abuses from pre-Reform days hung on. And as late as the 'nineties Lord Alfred Douglas informs me, there was a Fellow of one college, Fellow by right of family connection not of learning, who had survived the Reforms and who had never been known to teach the undergraduates anything but how not to carry their drink. Even after the war there were a few survivals. A clergyman who lived in Scotland kept a suite of fine panelled rooms in his college which he was not known to have visited for fifteen years. Undergraduates meanwhile were boarded out even after their first year in the college.

You may wonder what has happened to these dons of the old sort, dons who can have nothing to do with the word "donnish." University Reform from outside drove many of them into obscurity. They were despised in those common rooms where once they cracked jokes and laid down good vintages for future generations of their kind. They saw young men who spoke a different language from their own, who had the ill manners to discuss academic studies during meals, who called the old generation "abuses," who left the college for the long vacation and went on "reading parties" to various parts of Europe. They saw these young men getting friendly with undergraduates—and under-graduates who had no birth, no shooting to invite one to, no knowledge of a good wine, undergraduates who were merely likely to do well under the ridiculous new examination systems everyone seemed to set such store by. Little wonder that they cursed the name of Cyril Jackson, Dean of Christ Church at the beginning of the nineteenth century and pre-cursor of the world of alphas, betas, and gammas, first and second class brains, by which *fetiches* subsequent heads of colleges were to earn reputations as great Victorian educationalists. Now it was all education, but the old dons thought the younger ones had mistaken knowledge for education. They liked a good fellow better than a sound scholar.

There is a pathetic story of one of those last abuses who lingered on despised and a little tipsy to the beginning of this century. No one noticed him and he became so morose that he used to "sport his oak" and refuse to be seen even by his scout. One day, after no one had heard of him for three weeks, it was decided that perhaps he was ill. A scout was sent to knock on his oak. But either the double door was too thick or the old don was deafer than usual. There was no answer and the oak was broken down and the inner door burst open. The scout found his master on the floor; he had been dead a fort-night. The pathetic part of the story is (though it may not be true) that the old don left his beautiful collection of silver and his con-siderable private income "to —— College, because I have no one else to whom to leave it."

Few Fellows of reformed Oxford can afford to leave anything to the college which has been endowed, to a considerable extent, by those poor old abuses whom they despised. The young dons have wives and families in their North Oxford villas. The old ones were wedded only to their colleges. The monastic tradition died hard. Now little survives but the college buildings to tell us that the old Oxford was organized on monastic lines.*

A DON LOOKS AT HIS FELLOWS

I am afraid I am not in sympathy with Mr. Cheap, the author of the clever paper on his own Senior Common room, and which he has allowed me to print in this book. Obviously it would be ill-mannered of me to say I do not like him, especially after his kindness. But I think it only fair—and that I say, with the essential fairmindedness one associates with Oxford University—to fill in some of the gaps which Mr. Cheap has made.

You will read, if you get through Mr. Cheap's paper, of Mr. Tremaine and Mr. Pusey Pyx. They are particular friends of mine, and Mr. Cheap has underestimated them. Personally I have found the people he selects for especial praise "H. J." the wit, Mr. Snugg, Buffy Bounce, the Rev. Fence and Harry Ringworm, particularly repulsive.

Mr. Cheap has made but slight reference to dons in colleges other than his own. Now I would like to speak my mind. Some of my best friends are dons: they have been loyal to me in times of trouble: generous, hospitable, amusing: I do not want readers to go away with the impression that all dons are like those egotistical brutes mentioned in Mr. Cheap's paper. Thank goodness, all are not. Thank goodness there are some dons who are cultivated, not in the specialist sense; who are educated, but not entirely by the Beta and Gamma standards of the

---

* I should add here, that the bedroom of a bachelor don living in college has a distinctly monastic appearance. The sitting room may be large, thick-carpeted, hung with reproductions of modern art between the many book cases: there may be a smell of Turkish cigarettes and sherry. Open the door of the bedroom and you will see a bare, draughty little room with an iron bedstead an untidy chest of drawers and an old fashioned wash hand stand.

schools; who are capable of inspiring undergraduates; who remain detached even in the social martyrdom of some Senior Common Rooms. To these dons I would dedicate Mr. Cheap's paper, fully aware that Mr. Cheap will be yellow with resentment. This note will earn me Mr. Cheap's undying enmity. I do not care. This is my book, even though Mr. Cheap has written part of it. Mr. Cheap's friends are not mine. I prefer to make some attempt to retain my Oxford friends even at the cost of the acquaintance of Mr. Cheap.

The paper which follows was read to the S.E.E.C. (St. Ervan's Essay Club) and I was privileged to hear it as a guest of the Club to which I was invited by an undergraduate member in return for tea with Cornish cream at Ye Aldgate Tea Shoppe. Mr. Cheap's handwriting is not easy to read, so I took the precaution of making shorthand notes of his paper from which this is transcribed.

I am only sorry that Mr. Cheap gives no account of himself. In extenuation of what I have already said about him, I should add that though in his late 'fifties, he is still at heart a boy, with all a boy's enthusiasm for things St. Ervan.

*   *   *

Boys, light up your pipes and shove the cocoa cups on the trouser press, spread yourselves out over the bed-sitter, draw up the pouffe, huddle round the gas-ring.

You have seen the different types of dons there are; the old Professor of Comparative Palaeontology who bicycles down the Banbury Road once a week wearing a speckled straw hat and Evangelical clothes, in order to deliver his mythical lecture to a mythical audience but really to get a few things for his wife at Grimbly Hughes': Mr. Clack who keeps the Common room accounts so accurately and whose neat writing

Outside St. John's College.

and underlinings in different coloured inks are so admirable an expression of his personality; finally our friend Bill Bedstraw, whom I am happy to see with us to-night, who is just like you and me, a jolly chap with flannel bags and, I am glad to see, the college tie. Well, it takes all sorts to make a world doesn't it?

I think, since I am reading you a paper, we had better use the deductive method. I will paint the ideal don first, and we will then proceed to the facts. Of course before so distinguished company as this, I must be careful in my choice of words. I don't mean *ideal* in the philosophical sense, which would imply that the ideal don is the don who is not there, though you will pardon me continuing this delightfully Oxford joke into saying that we might almost—I say *almost*—take ideal in its philosophical as well as its colloquial sense. (Loud laughter and bangings of Freeman Hardy and Willis, Lotus, Delta and Phiteesi wear.) But it is my intention to portray at the outset, the perfect don. What, or rather who, is the perfect don?

We will see at once that this refers us further back into an enquiry into what is the perfect education? Now I hardly think we need have a discussion in this place on that vexed topic. You are expecting a paper on dons. But even if I were to elaborate on the educational theme— *sed quidnam Pamphilum exanimatum video?*—would we not be led into considering what is the perfect University? And would we not be conveyed back further into a consideration as to whether our present day universities are necessary at all? *Vide, quanti apud me sis?* I will not venture on such dangerous ground.

So by a process of ratiocinative inductive deduction (pardon my apparent unreasonableness, Goldwart, or would I be more correct in saying unreasonability, Professor Wyld? You will be able to correct me here.) I have found that it is not possible to paint the perfect don, after all. *Le Monsieur a barbe blanche* that tutor of whom you might well say

A Doctor of Divinity and a Chorister.

κρείσσων γαρ ἦσθα μηκέτ᾽ ὢν ἢ ὢν τυφλός, the other end of the pole, the young man just elected to the Senior Common Room of whose wits we might say in the West-Midland that they serve our argument "With a borelych by the bende by ye halme,"—whatever we regard as our perfect don, is not, I take it, the perfect don of our group mind. So far so good. Our argument flows "luce ridens calculorum, flore pictus herbido" if Tiberianus will forgive me.

VIVA VOCE

And now, gentlemen, if you will allow the laughter to subside, I will sum up my argument so far. There is no perfect don. To the perfect perfect, all things . . . and vice-versa. We must leave this frigid valley and proceed to dons as they are. What could I do better, than illustrate my theme by taking one by one the members of the Senior Common Room of our own college? Perhaps a fusion of all the noble qualities of the men depicted below, will result in that for which we vainly strive.

I think few people will find much to quarrel with in our WARDEN. Though he lives in the midst of us in a house which has, I am told, the best garden and the largest drawing room in Oxford, he remains a pattern to all the generations which have been up during his forty-seven years of Wardenship, of the cultivated recluse. There are not many men alive to-day who remember those stirring times when Trout was elected to the Wardenship. But I have had the story from those who do, and it is worth recording.

At that time, there were two very brilliant fellows, one a senior man —you may remember his name, those of you who do Critical Exegesis, he was Dr. Buster. If incisive scholarship allied to excessive seniority ever deserved the highest office the college has to bestow, those qualities were united in the character of Dr. Buster. In lay, as well as clerical circles, he was considered the likely candidate. Of the other famous fellow, J. B. Keaton, it is needless for me to speak. His witty verses, his contributions to philological criticism and his tragic death at the early age of fifty-seven on the slopes of Ben Nevis, have all alike immortalized his name. His was easily the most dominant personality in the Senior Common room at the time, and it was only his connection with Modern Languages which argued against him.

Faced with the choice of one or other of these brilliant men, the electing fellows were, if I may put it bluntly, in a fix.

Thus it came about that Alfred Trout, one of the younger fellows, and not supposed to live long, was elected by way of compromise. Trout was even then of a retiring disposition, and beyond the fact that he had published a short and valuable thesis on $2\pi\rho^2$ in the *Mathematical Quarterly*, little was known of him. But the Fellows thought, very rightly, that a mathematician would make an excellent man of business, and a man of business is invaluable as the head of a great college. Mr. Trout has published nothing since he has been Warden and on paper perhaps, his record will not appear outstanding. But we have in Mr. Trout one of the only heads of colleges, in fact almost *the* only head of a College, who would probably be capable, if called upon, of auditing the college accounts.

When the result of the election was known, Keaton took his defeat like a gentleman. He retired from active life in the college, gave up tutoring and lecturing and identified himself more and more with University Business. He was one of the prime leaders in the University's Senior Common Room Reconstruction Commission appointed by Sir Henry Campbell-Bannerman.

Dr. Buster very naturally retired to one of the college livings which at that time fell vacant. He retains the increment from his fellowship and his rooms in college are always open to him, though it is now twenty years since he has visited us. He lives the retired life of a country incumbent, doing as much good, no doubt, in his way, as he did in those days when he was a dominant force in Critical Exegesis. Of course, Dr. Buster is on the old foundation.

It is not now permitted for a non-resident fellow to retain his rooms in college unoccupied for more than three years.

I suppose it is natural to proceed from the Warden to the DEAN. You have all met Mr. Polkinghorne. He has a great gift for friendship.

He has almost an alpha mind into the bargain. His good looks and charm of manner have caused him to be known as "The popular Dean of St. Ervans" to the University at large. Perhaps he is not absolutely to be trusted by those who are inclined to impose on what appears to be his good nature. But the Dean, you will appreciate, has to keep in with all sections—with Junior as well as Senior Common Rooms and this is no light task.

And now, what of your CHAPLAIN, The Rev. A. Fence? Well, I think we must all approve him. To those of you who hold atheistic or militantly agnostic views, he is the soul of courtesy. Old Tony Fence as we called him when I was an undergraduate, was always a cheery chap. That cheeriness he still possesses: everyone knows his jolly greetings especially early in the morning, when you are on the way from ekker to brekker before nine o'clock lecker. "Nice day Catchpole!" "Fine morning Crowe!" "Jolly to be alive, Cavendish!" It doesn't matter who you are, Captain of Boats, Hockey Captain, President of the OUDS, or just an ordinary well-born undergraduate—you'll get a cheery greeting from Tony Fence. Those of you who are in the Church of England, may be wondering quite what religious opinions our Chaplain holds. There is nothing ritualistic, nothing "spikey" about him. He is definitely not "Anglo-Catholic". At the same time there is nothing Ultra-Protestant about him. I doubt whether old Tony Fence would commit himself to any party. I remember I once asked him, "Tell me, Tony, are you High, Low, or Central Church?" "I am none of them" was his reply. "But I am, I hope, a good churchman."

SENT DOWN?

Some of you may remember that our last Chaplain, Mr., or, as he liked to be called, "Father" Cotta, had rather pronounced views. Attempts were made—and I say it with all due respect to Mr. Cotta who, I feel sure, was a sincere man—to bother the heads of our youth with the "spiritual life" "mysticism" and "fasting Communion" and other somewhat debatable things. At a College meeting, we Senior Fellows felt obliged to ask him to resign. I feel sure that Mr. Cotta feels himself more at home with his "asceticism" in the college living (it is a **very** small one, but was the only one vacant at the time) of St. Barnabas, Bermondsey. Probably the people of Bermondsey will obtain more benefit from his ministration to their "spiritual lives" than a pack of healthy minded youngsters who want to acquire the learning obtainable at a great University like Oxford.

The Chaplain before Mr. Cotta, was perhaps rather too much to the other extreme. He was a Mr. Bag, and though a learned man, a *very* learned man, he was not ideally suited to a college chaplaincy. He denied the divinity of Our Lord, and refused to celebrate the Holy Communion on the ground that it was an unnecessary appendage to a faith which had progressed since the Middle Ages. He was what you might term an advanced modernist. Naturally the choir and organist objected to the omission of a service which they render very well "sung"—though

St. Ervan's Sung Communion is not in any sense ritualistic, being at 12.30 on the third Sunday in the month—and a College meeting was held. We were able to offer Mr. Bag the important City Church of St. Botolph Barbican with a net income of £3,200 p.a. There he will have the leisure to pursue his life of scholarship.

But our present Chaplain, I am happy to say, holds no religious opinions at all. "The only spiritual matter you will have to bother about Tony," I said to him in private conversation soon after we had elected him, "is college spirit." Tony Fence is of course, an old St. Ervans man, though he may not be a book worm, he comes of a fine old family with traditions behind it.

Now I come to the enviable task of describing my colleagues and it is inevitable that I start with a description of the Senior Fellows. Dr. Buster who is non-resident and on the old foundation we have already considered. Some of my more flippant colleagues have had the temerity to nickname him "The Abuse," but this is hardly fair to one who, in his day, may have been very famous.

Our Senior Member of Common Room is Professor Harpoon, Emeritus Professor of Mediaeval Ichthyology. He is a married man and lives in retirement in North Oxford. For the past thirty-two years there have been no students of Mediaeval Ichthyology so that the Professor has been able to apply himself entirely to research in that important subject. He very rarely comes to the college and on his few visits he has never been known to address a word either to his colleagues or to the undergraduates. He is, if I may say so, a shy man not given to conversation. But his vote is most useful at College meetings. Recently he has become paralysed in both arms so that he cannot vote at meetings in the way we generally do, which is by a show of hands. He is, however, able to raise his feet and he has been prevailed upon to raise his right foot as a token of assent when his vote is required. There is little else I can say about

Professor Harpoon, since very little is known about him, but we all respect his learning for Oxford is a city where learning always receives its due.

One of the cleverest of our Fellows is Mr. Snugg who is known among you, I am told, as "The Snake." It is always a sign of popularity for a man to have a nickname and I am glad to hear he has one with you.

Mr. Snugg is a Lecturer in Law and those of you who do law will appreciate his quiet cynicism. That smooth voice is the mouthpiece of a shrewd and penetrating mind. At college meetings when the fate of some erring undergraduate is in the balance, Mr. Snugg puts up a fine case for the prosecution.

Many undergraduates who are of little interest to the college— that is to say those who choose their friends from other colleges, who refuse to join in the college games, who take up "art" and acting and university journalism, who waste their parents' money entertaining friends to large meals in their rooms, who cut Mr. Clack's tutorials—

PLUCKED !

many undergraduates of this sort have been sent down for good, thanks to the able researches of Mr. Snugg into their private lives.

Mr. Snugg himself, besides being an acute lawyer, has a great admiration for actresses and women film stars whose portraits adorn the walls of his sumptuous rooms. He is frequently in London, but on business connected indirectly with the college. People have told me that he looks more like a business man than a don. And I have replied, "well why should not a don be a business man?"

On occasions Mr. Snugg has brought actresses to the college: a strange sight for us monastic creatures.

If Mr. Snugg is suave, I might almost say feline, what a contrast with him we have in Buffy Bounce, "Buffy" as he is called all over the college. Who doesn't know "Buffy"? and who, who knows him, doesn't love him? Reginald Bounce is his proper name, though one forgets that "Buffy" has a Christian name at all—somehow "Buffy" suits so well that round, jovial, red-faced fellow whom you may see any time in the summer trotting down in shorts, his bald head gleaming above his white sweater, on his way to toggers or boggers playing leap froggers with an undergraduate, his great boisterous laugh swinging like a gust of wind up into the elm trees of Christ Church Walk. And in the winter months, there's "Buffy" again, every afternoon, shorts and sweater on, legging it to the squash court with some chosen companion from among your number.

It was a toss up whether "Buffy" was to be games master at a great public school—he got his blue for rugger, his blue for hockey, his half blue for fencing, his quarter blue for real tennis, his blue for rowing and his Leander tie—it was a toss up, I say, whether "Buffy" went as games coach to—well I must be frank—to Marlborough or came here as rowing coach. His career at the University was outstanding. He won a scholarship to B.N.C. for rugger and then, after an unparalleled career in athletics, he also achieved a sound Third in Law. With a degree and an athletic record, he was all a college could require and we straightway offered him a fellowship at St. Ervan's.

I think we were justified. The tutorial part of "Buffy's" life is not

The Tower of the Five Orders (1612–19) showing only the two topmost of them.

Magdalen College, New Buildings, 1733.

Headington Stone in Lincoln College.

its most important, so we have put him on to teaching English literature, and though he is no pedant, he is capable of taking great pains.
Those who want to go more elaborately into English literature may
take tutorials outside the college, though naturally we do not encourage
that form of disloyalty.

Two years after he became a Fellow, St. Ervan's was Head of the
River, top in Toggers, the winning college at hockey, and two of our
men played real tennis for the University. "Buffy" is feeling his age a
bit now and so we have brought Sandy McGregor along to help him.

There are two things "Buffy" will not tolerate. They are slackness
in any form whether in work or games, and disloyalty to the college.
Sometimes, perhaps, "Buffy" goes a little too far in his enthusiasm.
An affected ass who wrote poetry—and has since made a name for
himself, I am told, among the intelligentsia of Bloomsbury—objected
to being roped in to row for our seventh boat on the river. He appeared
for rowing dressed as a Greek soldier in a white kilt. "Buffy" did not
say anything at the time, but I was there and I noticed he fixed his eye
on that kilt. After rowing practice, he asked the poet to come to tea.
The poet, thinking he had made a conquest over an athlete, accepted.
When he got him in his room, "Buffy" bent that poet double, lifted
up his kilt and gave him the biggest tanning he had ever had in his
life, with his bare hand. Of course the college, dons and undergraduates alike, were delighted; but we had to give "Buffy" an official
rebuke at the next college meeting, though, it must be confessed, that
we gave it with a twinkle in our eyes.

The remarkable thing about "Buffy" is his delight in college spirit.
To many old St. Ervan's men, St. Ervan's is "Buffy". There's not a
wine club, dining club—no nor even an essay club—which "Buffy"
does not attend. He would be here to-night were it not that the
Rowing Committee has a meeting. I have even heard it said (tell it

not in Gath!) that "Buffy" has been known to join in the breaking up of the rooms of "aesthetes" accused of disloyalty to the college, after a Bump supper.

Next comes the Bishop Proudie Professor of Comparative Numismatics, Professor Scurf. His bicycle with its basket of books on the handlebars, is a familiar object leaning up against the porter's lodge for long periods of the day. During the many years that he has been here, Professor Scurf has never missed a meal at high table. He even has his Christmas dinner in college when some of the staff are held back from their holidays to provide him with whatever he may want.

He is a methodical man and many undergraduates are said to set their watches in the morning by his regular appearance shuffling down from his rooms through the cloisters.

You, who are members of the Junior Common Room, have no opportunity of appreciating his mordaunt wit. But it is a real intellectual treat to his colleagues when he and our great "H.J." have a sparring match after the port.

"Read the latest Dornford Yates, Professor?"

"I have not yet given myself that pleasure, H. J., doubtless you, as a philosopher, have to keep in touch with all the latest authorities."

"Come, come, Professor. That is hardly fair. I am, *nescio-quid*, able for a moment to allow myself the leisure of reading lay literature."

"Lay literature. Is it something to do with poultry? Enlighten me, Mr. Domestic Bursar."

"I think H. J. is referring to a humorous writer. Mr. Yates rejoices in that reputation."

"Thank you. Thank you. No doubt you are referring to a philosopher of Humour." It is well known at High Table that the Professor possesses the largest collection of Dornford Yates' novels in the college.

"Not at all, Professor. I am referring to the humour of philosophy."

"Surely humour, H. J., is an affection of the will. As far as I recollect— pardon a blundering Numismatist attempting to correct the University Lecturer in Experimental Philosophy—as far as I recollect Schopenhauer defines it as such."

"No, Professor, that is his definition of joy. He says joy and sorrow are not ideas of the mind."

"Too subtle, too subtle, H. J. I must accuse myself of what Theophrastus calls ἀναισθησία καὶ βραδυτὴς ψυχῆς."

And so on till well towards midnight. You may be sure that when the Professor and H.J. are in form, very few of us leave the Common room until they have finished. I sometimes think their memorable duels should be recorded on one of those instruments for taking down conversations. The name escapes me for the moment.

Too often we are reduced to puzzling together in a joint attempt to solve *The Times* Crossword and for this purpose the latest edition of *Encylopaedia Britannica* has been purchased out of the library funds and installed in the Senior Common Room. Even dons are human.

And now for "H.J." I expect you were wondering when I was going to come to him. I am glad he is not here to-night to witness my inadequate attempts to portray his arresting personality. "H.J." does not associate himself with undergraduates nor undergraduate clubs, so I knew I would be spared the humiliation of having his incisive and logical mind taking in the substance of this paper and dissecting it ruthlessly afterwards.

H. J. Robinson, the University Lecturer in Experimental Philosophy —though I should add that he rarely lectures, devoting his time to more profitable pursuits than what he calls "casting his imitation pearls before real swine"—H. J. Robinson is probably the most brilliant man at Oxford at present. He took a first in Greek before the war and was immediately made a fellow of St. Ervan's where he has remained ever since.

His physical appearance perhaps misleads. His black suit which he is said never to have changed since he was elected to his Fellowship, is the only vestige left of his clerical calling. For it is well known that H.J. took orders in the same delightful spirit of cynicism with which he answers his colleagues at high table. He is very near-sighted and this accounts for the fact that he often seems to stare rudely at undergraduates and to cut his acquaintances, though it has been remarked that when he meets acquaintances of the opposite sex, such as the wives of his colleagues, he is totally blind. But then H.J. is a "character" and we must permit him his foibles.

Fundamentally H.J. is a kindhearted man. As an instance of this let me quote the famous story of the don and the dead undergraduate. You all know the tale. H.J. was a tutor at the time and it happened that one of his less brilliant pupils died during the term. In his letter of condolence to the parents H.J. said "But you may take consolation from the fact that your son would undoubtedly have failed to get through Pass Moderations at the end of this term."*

With all his kindheartedness, there is one failing which H.J. will never pardon and that is lack of intelligence. He has been known to sit in complete silence at meals with those of his colleagues who have houses in North Oxford and who have asked him out. No doubt, he has thought the hostess not his intellectual equal or he has disapproved of one of the guests.

Once a colleague whom I forbear to mention brought his father to high table as a guest. This colleague was no favourite of H.J. and it so happened that the father found himself next to H.J. Someone effected an introduction. "This is Mr.——, the father of ——."

"Indeed" said H.J. "if this is a gentleman who has been able to put up with —— for all ——'s life, then I cannot put up with such a gentle-

---

* This story comes, in a slightly varied form, from J. W. E. Russell's *Reminiscences*.

man for five minutes." And he forthwith addressed no further word to him during the whole meal. Many of us were intensely amused at this brilliant, if cruel, retort and those of us who were not well disposed to —— watched with no little interest the discomfiture of ——'s father.

It is an idiosyncrasy of H.J. that he dislikes members of any other college—an idiosyncrasy if such it can be called, which most of us share. H.J. allows his prejudice to approximate to mania. He always reads a book at high table when he finds himself next to a guest. At one time he was taken unawares and a particularly learned old gentleman from another college was placed next to him. H.J. had known him in his youth, but apparently they had not been sympathetic. H.J. cast one withering glance at his neighbour, turned to the waiter and said, "Fox, fetch me the current number of the *Hibbert Journal* from the Senior Common Room at once." This he proceeded to read for the rest of the meal.*

Dear old H.J. I dread to think what our College would be like without him. I notice that he has taken up an undue proportion of this paper so now we must float down from these Olympic heights.

There is Mr. Clack the Domestic Bursar. I have had occasion to

---

* Lest anyone should think Mr. Cheap exaggerates the respect for H. J. at St. Ervan's, let me quote this extraordinary passage from Oxford (Spring 1936). The article is called *Balliol in the 'eighties*, by J. A. Spender. It contains a description of Jowett written presumably in all earnestness and meant, I must believe, to show what a great man J. was. "During the whole four years I was up I scarcely passed a term without being invited to a solitary meal with him, either breakfast or dinner. The time passed in almost complete silence. Now and again I used to venture an embarrassed remark, but as likely as not the reply would be, 'You wouldn't have said that if you had stopped to think', and after that silence more glacial still he dismissed me with a brief 'Good morning'.

"Then there were those formidable occasions when, six together, you read essays to him on philosophical subjects he had set, and again silence was his weapon. You read your essay feeling a warm glow at the eloquence of its closing passage. Sometimes he rewarded you with a brief 'Good essay' or 'Fair essay', but there were other occasions when he looked at you for an interminable minute and then slowly shifted his gaze to your neighbour and said 'Next essay, please'."

The tales of this great man and inspiring tutor are, of course, feeble beside those about Mark Pattison, the Rector of Lincoln, who was another don, the soul of courtesy and sympathy with youth.

refer already to the neat hand writing, coloured inks, and general efficiency of Mr. Clack. Mr. Clack is the only member of our Common Room to take a Second in Theology. For this reason we have found it impossible to make him a Fellow, but he proves himself invaluable in other ways. He keeps the College accounts with impeccable accuracy. Not only this, but Mr. Clack takes more undergraduates for tutorials than any other don. We allow him to take as many pupils as he can manage since the money he makes by this means somewhat compensates for the amount he loses in not being a Fellow. There are those who have told me that they do not find Mr. Clack an inspiring tutor. May I take this opportunity of saying that the fault is more probably on the side of the pupil than that of the tutor? Mr. Clack cannot be expected to be able to keep up with the latest developments in the various subjects he teaches. He has not the time. Isn't it then a chance of there being a little give and take on the part of tutor and pupil? Besides, those of you who go to Mr. Clack for tutorials must remember that if he did not take you, other dons whose time is more fully occupied in research etc., might be obliged to waste their lives teaching undergraduates elementary subjects which can perfectly well be taught by someone of the admirable qualifications of Mr. Clack.

I must admit that Mr. Clack is quiet. A little precise, a hard worker, unfailingly patient, he yet does not pervade the college as dear old H.J. does. His calligraphy is well known to us all, but I wonder how many of you can recall what his voice is like, what he wears, or even what he looks like?

I will not spend long in discussing a man of very different character, Mr. Tremaine. I am afraid I do not know him. Therefore I think it would be unfair of me to say anything prejudicial. He is not a Fellow. We have seen to that, for Mr. Tremaine has a considerable income of his own and is in no need of the extra emolument. Unluckily for the college, Mr. Tremaine is one of those gentlemen whose interests and friends take him to other parts of the University. He has, I believe, a large collection of books of English colour plates, though what these have to do with the subject which the University pays him to teach (High Dutch) I am unable to discover. I have heard that he gives "exclusive" dinner parties in his rooms asking undergraduates, particularly those who display a deplorable lack of college spirit, to meet similar undergraduates from other colleges. Not only this, but certain dons (none, I am thankful to say, from St. Ervan's) and various rather unhealthy *litterateurs* from London have also attended these parties. H.J. and "Buffy" join forces in disapproving of this unfortunate tendency in Mr. Tremaine. He is said to be reckoned a connoisseur of food and wine and this, no doubt, is an admirable quality, but in these days of specialists, when we are safely able to leave the choice of what we eat or drink in the able hands of the Co-operative Societies such connoisseurship seems, to many of us, a waste of valuable time. He is the only member of the Senior Common Room whose presence causes several members to leave the room.

Mr. Tremaine has a large country house and, strange to say, he has never once invited a member of the St. Ervan's Senior Common Room to its sacred precincts. This slight a good many of us feel. I do not wish to imply that we bear animosity to Mr. Tremaine, we are, I hope, above caring about such petty indignities. But you will realize that Mr. Tremaine's behaviour precludes him from any advancement in University status. He has been Lecturer in High Dutch for the past ten years and Lecturer he will remain. He stands no chance of either a Fellowship or a Professorship. It is essential that senior members of the University should pull together.

Let us turn to a more familiar subject—Sandy McGregor. Sandy came up to St. Ervan's with a Polytechnic Scholarship. He hailed from braw bonnie Scotland as his patronymic implies. He is an out-standing example of what well-balanced industry and praiseworthy ambition may do. A remarkable thing about Sandy was that he became a good oar, rowing in the first boat. The only river Sandy had known before he came to Oxford was the Clyde.

To-day Sandy is an invaluable member of the College. He has hardly a trace of his Scotch accent; he is a good rowing coach and an experienced chemist. Of course, he is direct and bluff. The only thing we cannot understand about him is his friendship with Mr. Tremaine. He is a severe critic of any Englishmen whether from a public school or elsewhere. "Hard work and hard play" is Sandy's motto, and no excursions into any realms which are not the subject in hand. Sandy has studied chemistry all his life and what he does not know about it, no one knows. Naturally he has not had time to acquire that veneer of polite literature and good manners which some people are foolish enough to consider the essence of an Oxford education. Sandy is a specialist. He knows his subject and nothing more. The University should be composed of specialists. I think there are plenty of people at St. Ervan's and more still in other colleges, who might take a leaf out of Sandy's book. A little less dilettantism and a little more "knowledge" is what many men need. Except for the women examiners, Sandy is, as an examiner, the most penetrating and severe.

Sandy is a very genuine and sincere man. For instance when we have port in the Senior Common Room, Sandy always has cocoa specially made for him. At dinner at high table many of you may have noticed how Sandy always has a cup of tea when the rest of us are drinking Burgundy or Hock. Then Sandy objects to the principle of having rooms in college. He says they are too luxurious. So he lives in a back bedroom of a house down a turning off the Cowley Road and though this is rather a long way for his scout to come and look after him, we can all

In Broad Street.

appreciate the genuine feelings which make him choose the life of the people rather than the arid and snobbish setting of an ancient college.

Sandy belongs to only one undergraduate society and that is U.T.S. (University Trotskyist Society) which all undergraduates are rightly compelled to join.

Another prominent member of "The Trotter"* is our friend Bill Bedstraw whom I am glad to see here to-night. Bill is a remarkable man and I'm sure he won't mind my saying so. He did not let his public school interfere with his social conscience. Many a time when we were undergraduates together have I seen him pedalling down towards Cowley to a Boys' Club Cocoa Crush, scowling from his bicycle at those who were not doing their economic duty. Since then Bill has become Chairman of the Oxford Housing Estates Planning Board and, though he would be the last person to confess to a knowledge of town planning or such trivialities as aesthetics, he is an able and forceful chairman and has invented the slogan "A bathroom to every worker's bedroom".

Bill is to many of us the perfect younger don. Scarcely distinguishable from an ordinary undergraduate in his physical appearance and in his joviality, he yet has advanced further in political theory than any of us. Many of you have had hot muffins before Bill's gas-ring and munched them by the dozen through long and profitable arguments on the merits of Trotsky and Stalin. Bill has no time for humbug. He has no use for Christianity which he calls "white magic", and it is only on social occasions such as weddings, christenings and funerals, that he attends the services of the church. He has no use for our effete aristocracy, except insofar as it is useful to his social advancement.

> Left wings are more than coronets
> And double firsts than Norman blood.

* University slang for Trotskyist Society.

81

Outside Balliol College. Typical Oxford bicycle with a basket in front for educational books.

But I think the quality we most admire in Bill Bedstraw is the thoroughness with which he lives up to his principles. He it was who persuaded the College Steward to order all food from the Co-ops. He it is who is leader of the movement to turn college gardens into allotments so that each college may be self supporting during times of economic crisis: he it is who is attempting to do away with the laying down of vintage wines by college stewards: the reduction of a don's wages to 32s. a week: the establishment of cocoa-fountains in all quadrangles: the demolition of out of date buildings: the furtherance of industrial research: the industrialization of further research: the research into further industrialization: the economic use of social

A POPULAR YOUNG DON

studies: the study of social economic use: the use of economic &c.: the extension of the L.W.T.F.B. in the V.W.H. (Cricklade): the co-operation of the Amalgamated Artisans B of W.T.L.Z. (Huddersfield and N. Riding) with the Oxford Spare Parts Workers, W.T.Z.L.: the Harrod curve: the Permanent Way: the P.W.D.I.: N.U. of I.D.W.P., &c.

His books are well known to you all and his occasional letters to the *New Statesman* are masterpieces of profound reasoning. How often have we chuckled over *Britannicus Asseveratus*, *Left Wings over Headington*, *Theophrastus' Ideological Soviet*, *The Trial of Constitutionalism in the Face of Democratic Crisis: Oxford's International*.

Then think of the undergraduate clubs to which Bill belongs. President of "The Trotter": President of The Red Reading Club:

Organizer of the Boy Hikers' Group: Chairman, Communist Nature Rambles Society: Vice-President of the following clubs circle—Zix, Slash, Burst, Priam Group, Plato's Republicans, founder of Platonic University Campers.

Those of you who have attended Bill Bedstraw's discussion group which he holds weekly in Stewart's will realize what a vital bond Bill is between the less re-actionary sections of the town and enlightened university thought.

I now come to the last of the members of our Senior Common Room of whom I am able to treat in any detail. He is Harry Ringwurm. Those of you who have been to his softly-lit rooms will realize that he is a connoisseur of art. Etchings by Brangwyn look almost lost on the large panelling: a single reproduction of a Botticelli smiles down from above the mantelpiece and a della Robia placque hangs above his pipe rack. Despite his true appreciation of art, Harry does not let his taste nor his life go to extremes. He is a sound tutor and a great upholder of college spirit and college traditions. The college feels how invaluable it is to have a keen sound man at its meetings who also has aesthetic ability. When the new wing was to be added to St. Botolph's Buildings—an ungainly barrack-like affair of the eighteenth century containing large gloomy rooms with unnecessarily elaborate ceilings—it was Harry Ringwurm who advised us to get Sir James Butterfield, the great London architect. Together these two devised the lovely new addition to St. Botolph's Buildings which was opened by the Bishop of Winchester this term. It is Gothic without being inconvenient, moderne without being ultra modern, and though there are those who criticize its position on the main road where it is subject to traffic noises, I must ask you to remember that double windows have been inserted, at great expense, in all the rooms. We hope in time to pull down all the ugly and plain eighteenth century buildings in the college to substitute more work in this appropriate Moderno-Gothic style. The New Bodleian library buildings should be a model to all.

Harry Ringwurm besides being an able tutor and an art connoisseur, lives an active social life. When His Serene Highness the Emperor of China sent his son to St. Ervan's, Harry was one of the first to make the acquaintance of this charming young man and asked him to luncheon to meet those undergraduates he thought would be suitable companions for him such as Lord Porcorum, Lord Bicestershire, Sir Harley Wimpole and John Smash (Lord Pessimy's boy). Harry has the wonderful gift of being able to get on with all sorts and conditions of men and one will often find in his room some of the highest in the land, or I should say, in the college. There are those who accuse Harry of being a snob. But I would like to refute this charge. Harry has the knack of knowing the best people and of attracting them to his rooms. If this is snobbery, then I am a snob myself.

Harry Ringwurm's scholarship is light and easy. You all know how intensely amusing he can be. He is never better than when reading a paper to undergraduates. I remember the time when he proved in a singularly ingenious essay to the Junior Philological Circle, that Dr. Johnson was really Shakespeare and in the course of his argument proved that Dr. Johnson was a fool and Shakespeare no poet. It is this clever provocative power of self expression which so charms the undergraduates and sharpens their minds. In a way, one might say, it gives them the Oxford outlook.

There are, I am aware, other senior members, other of us dons in St. Ervan's, whom I have been unable to mention within the compass of a short paper. I can only dismiss them briefly, for they are members of St. Ervan's Senior Common Room who play only a small part in the college life.

Mr. Dandruff we see rarely nowadays, except at meal times. For the last seventeen years he has been engaged on his important book *Two Years of Richard II's Internal Policy* which I see announced by the Clarendon Press (170 pages: one illustration: £3 3*s*. net). We all look forward to another important contribution to British history from a St. Ervan's man.

Then there is Mr. Pusey-Pyx who lives, I fear, rather in the past. He has an income of his own which he spends, I am told, in charity, no doubt an admirable way of spending it. Though he lives in the college, he is a retiring man and takes little part in either senior or undergraduate life.

Mr. Henry Dim lives in North Oxford where he has a wife and large family. Mrs. Dim takes in post-graduates reading for a geography thesis. I am afraid I cannot remember what is Mr. Dim's subject, nor can any of my colleagues. As he hardly ever comes to the college, I have been unable to ask him.

Of course we have our quota of Honorary Fellows and they number some of the most distinguished men in the country. This list speaks for itself. Brigadier-General Sir Bartle Toop, a former Governor of the Society Islands; Lord Pinewood, who as Sir Elisha Pein, popular-ized synthetic vegetables and has since founded the Pinewood Chair of Research into Chemical Foodstuffs; Mr. Sussex Tankard, the poet; and, of course, the Rt. Hon. Arthur Rhomboid.

I have drawn a picture, *simalacrum immeritum*, but withal *honoris causa*, of the

TUTORIAL

THE HEAD COOK OF BRAZENFACE

little Republic, one might almost describe it as such, which we impose. ΜΗΔΕΙΣ ΑΓΕΩΜΕΤΡΗΤΟΣ ΕΙΣΤΩ. Perhaps some of you listening here to-night—you, for instance, Montmorency—may one day be privileged to join our numbers.

I have often heard dons criticized. Believe me they are too easy game and the criticism often comes from those who were disappointed in their University or who did not receive the inestimable benefit of a University education. I hope I have shown to-night, utinam vocem Ciceronis habui, the many sided excellence, the domus multiplex, of our Senior Common Room. We are none of us perfect and naturally we have our weak spots.

But I think that a man combining the modesty of our Warden, the industry of Mr. Clack, the gift of friendship of the Dean, the tolerance of the Chaplain, the erudition of Professor Scurf, the wit of "H.J.", the astuteness of Mr. Snugg, the keenness of "Buffy" Bounce, the down-rightness of Sandy McGregor, the enthusiasm and energy of Bill Bedstraw, the social sense of Harry Ringwurm and his taste, Professor Harpoon's courage, in the face of physical disability

—I think such a man, a veritable Odysseus, could never be found, even among the Senior Common Rooms of Oxford.

There is an old saying in the Isle of Man, where I come from, which goes "Cur dou yn sollan, my sailliu" and it means "Give to me the salt, if you please", or in polite language "Kindly pass the cruet". Let me suggest that you savour your criticism of dons. Bear with our shortcomings. We aren't such bad chaps after all, just ordinary chaps like you who have been listening to me to-night, but we happen to be brain boxes into the bargain.

I notice I have exceeded the allotted time with this paper and there will be no time for questions. Indeed those of you who are in digs will have to hurry up if you are to get home, before lock-up. Well, I must be going myself. Montmorency, are you coming my way?

Chapter Four

COLLEGE SERVANTS

" . . . there are good scouts as well as wicked; and—if the Fresh-man did but know—he would choose his rooms entirely by the scout on whose stairs they are, and not by the furniture. Later on, he will change his rooms solely to get on a stair where there is a reputed jewel of a scout." *Oxford Ways* by Blair. [Basil Blackwell, 1925.]

*   *   *

"YOUR ROOMS ARE ON THE
SECOND FLOOR, SIR"

The host of college servants is bigger than that of a Senior Common Room and almost as vast as that of the undergraduates. There is the steward who seems the most import-ant with, if he is a good steward, his taste in wine and his understanding of scouts and undergraduates. There is the college porter with his incor-ruptibility, and, if he is to retain his job, his memory for faces.

There is the chef. For many years Queen's College had the best cooking. I do not know whether this is still so. There was a rumour that the chef was sent to France during vacations to learn new dishes. The best cellar, now that the celebrated Gynes has retired from Magdalen where he laid down superb vintages, is said to be Pembroke.

The Oxford meal in most colleges is all too familiar and most of the food is tinned.

Tea was not, until recently, considered an important function except in North Oxford. It is a significant social commentary that Balliol College specializes in teas.

Dinner is not a social function of importance except among dons and for Bump Suppers where people concentrate more on getting drunk than appreciating wine and food.

There is no really good restaurant in Oxford, the nearest approach to one being The George where Madame et Monsieur Ersham as host and hostess are known to generations of undergraduates. Next to The George I would recommend the Regency calm of the Golden Cross. But all this is purely temporary advice. Undergraduate clubs vary, equally with restaurants, in their food.

Indeed the link between food, wine and culture, so strong till before the Great War, is now very weak indeed. Where food is appreciated, the appreciation is generally something precious and savouring of class consciousness, but the majority of undergraduates are content with beer, cocoa and the tinned food of colleges and restaurants. Indeed the restaurants in the town cater just as much for the Motopolis as they do for undergraduates and their food is of the usual tasteless sort of the and/or variety, four courses for 1s. 3d. not including coffee.

Of course the town abounds in dainty tea shops where the cakes are of quite a high standard.

I bring this disquisition of food into the chapter on College Servants, because it is in the matter of luncheon parties in college that your scout comes up to scratch or fails.

Scout.

If your scout likes you, he will take trouble for you. He will get in other scouts (whom you must tip) if the luncheon is to be a big one. In my own college, I found the scouts more interesting and more efficient and human than the majority of the dons. That some scouts are rapacious, I will not deny—but then their wages are not so high as a don's. Despite their human failings, the college servants (and by this I mean chiefly the scouts who look after undergraduates residing in college) are the people who set the standard for the college.

A good scout can coax a man from greed or parsimony to an appreciation of modest comfort; he can over-awe a cocoa-drinking don; he can sum up a flashy bounder; he is, if he is a really

SCOUT AND SCHOLAR

good scout, something of a snob, not necessarily in a matter of titles, but in food, drink and good manners. He is a distinctly conservative person, considering his wages.

Stories about scouts are endless, and unnecessary here. What is necessary, is some appreciation of the immense amount of work they have to do. George Colman the Younger, who was up at Ch: Ch: in 1780 describes the duties of a scout and it will surprise the more left wing among us to notice that his duties are but slightly different now. "He undergoes the double toil of Boots at a well-frequented Inn, and a Waiter at Vauxhall, in a successful season.—After coat-brushing, shoe-cleaning, and message-running,* in the morning, he has upon an average, half-a-dozen supper parties† to attend, in the same night and

* The message-running is now less considerable.
† For these substitute three lunch parties. Scouts do not get teas for undergraduates.

An undergraduate's bedroom.

at the same hour;—shifting a plate here, drawing a cork there, running to and fro, from one set of chambers to another,—and almost solving the Irishman's question of 'how can I be in two places at once, *unless I was a bird?*' And, when he considers the quantity of work he has to slur over, with small pay, among his multitude of masters, it serves, perhaps, as a salve to his conscience, for his petty larcenies." It is hardly true of scouts that they lay in for Freshmen as they did for George Colman, jnr., "—wine, tea, sugar, coals, candles, bed and table linen—with many useless *et cætera*, which they *told* me I wanted; —charging me for everything full half more than they had paid, and then purloining from me full half of what they had sold". In some college a little profit is made on coals, table linen and a few etcetera: small blame to the scouts. During term time, theirs is a hard life, especially if at the end of it, no tip is forthcoming, and in these days of state-subsidized education and small allowances tips are smaller.

Up till now I have only considered scouts from the outside point of view.

Do you, Professor Scurf, know what that polite man who brings your hot water in the morning thinks of you and your learning? He will not forget the many times you have made him stay up after term— yes, even on Christmas Day—to minister to your wants when he was looking forward to Christmas dinner at home down beyond St. Clement's with his children back for this day in the year. And you, Mr. Chaplain, with your tolerance. Are you not a bit of an autocrat?

And "H.J.", the college wit, the man for happy high table phrases! Your scout knows what you do with those mysterious hours given to research. He knows what your temper is like in the morning.

Poor Mr. Clack, meagre domestic bursar, with all those pupils and that continual work. You do at least pride yourself on the fact that you are a don: you can fluff out your gown and let it flutter in the wind before admiring visitors and townsmen. But your scout sees through your little vanity. He knows the tiny tip you can afford him at the end of term, knows he got that gown for you cheap from a retiring fellow

"AND THIS IS WHERE HE'LL KEEP HIS COAL"

and, when he cleans out your monastic bedroom, he finds those loving letters from your old mother thanking you for the money you must have sent her.

And Mr. Snugg, shrewd business man, the one with the ladies, so fussy about those many pin-stripe suits, so particular about your shirts. You are more than a whole staircase full of 'em, to your scout. He knows that you count the number of cigars in your box and mark in red ink the level of the whiskey. Do you think he likes you? No more than anyone else does.

And you, Mr. Cheap, who read that revealing paper on St. Ervan's. Your scout has unlocked the skeletons. Yes, they come rattling out and clattering down the staircase every time you leave that copy of Victor Margerite by your bedside or inadvertently forget to put back *The History of the Rod* bound up as *Virgil*, on your shelves.

And Buffy Bounce, the sports' enthusiast, the college-spiritist. You, too, cannot hide your little failings from your scout.

The trouble Sandy MacGregor causes his scout has been referred to already. But Bill Bedstraw, the political theorist, the live wire, the reformer—what does your scout think of you? Does he tire of carrying those many repeat orders for crumpets up your twisting stair? Does he find your rooms deplorably untidy? Does he curse you when he has to brush the tobacco ash and coffee stains out of your carpet? to remove the crumbs from the upholstery? to leave the endless periodicals in the picturesque abandon you like to see them in? Maybe, he does, Bill, old boy. Maybe he, too, notices that your many outside activities give you little time to do the work you are so well paid to do. And I don't think he likes all those visitors who come to your rooms—though, theoretically of course, he is one of our great big brotherhood—I have

noticed how gingerly he hangs up Councillor Gaspipe's mackintosh. Enough of this class consciousness. It's Harry Ringwurm that none of the scouts can abide. His finicky fussiness about his artistic furniture. Pretending he knows about food and wine—as though he knew any more than half the undergraduates he asks to his occasional lunch parties.

LOOKING ROUND THE DEAR OLD
COLLEGE

I'm afraid the scouts are a little old fashioned. I'm afraid they don't think Bill Bedstraw a good advertisement for Communism. I'm afraid they like Mr. Tremaine and Mr. Pusey Pyx better than the rest.

Perhaps when the social life of the college is properly adjusted and scouts are allowed to read for degrees and give lectures and talk about politics and art—in fact when the sizarship system is thoroughly re-established, not just half established as it is now, perhaps then they will get the right outlook on Bill Bedstraw and all the rest of Mr. Cheap's friends, and despise Mr. Tremaine and Mr. Pyx for the old fogeys they are.

But till that day, I am afraid scouts will judge the men they look after rather by the schools from which they come. I am afraid they will lump all grammar schools and secondary schools and polytechnics under one head. That is to say, the majority of them will. I am afraid

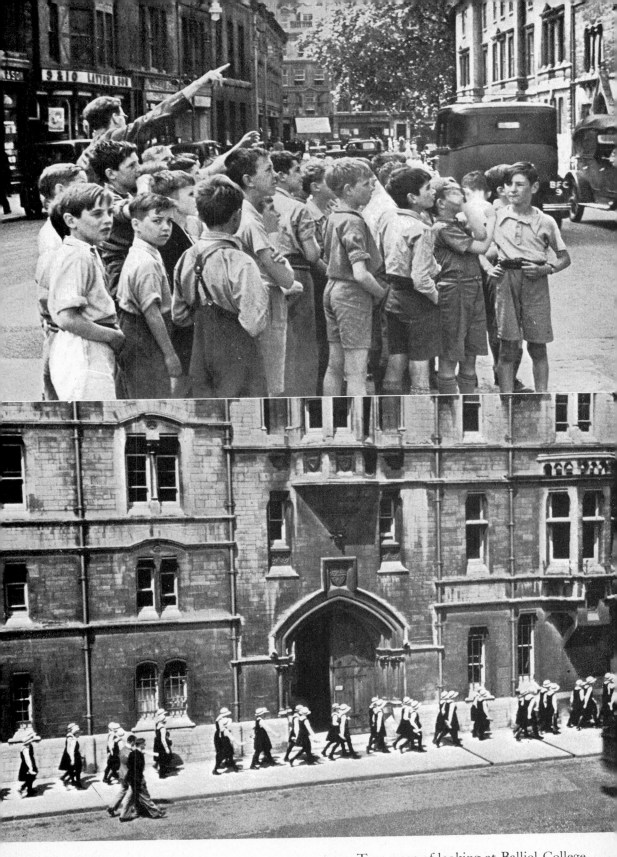

Two ways of looking at Balliol College.

In the High Street.

they will like to see wine flowing instead of cocoa; half a dozen oysters instead of a dozen digestive biscuits: a young man stupified with his first experience of mixed drinks instead of exhilarated with his first reading of *Das Kapital*.

They will continue to take an interest in the personalities of the men they liked: they will follow their careers when they have gone down far more closely and less enviously than the dons. Those little houses, those little yellow and red brick villas in near-Eastern Oxford, smaller, yet somehow like the larger villas to which the married dons migrate in North Oxford, will still be spotlessly clean. Still in the unused parlour will hang portraits of past undergraduates, great dukes or great drunks, or great men: and photographs of the grind: and of some, but of oh how few, of the dons. And above all a college crest?

And what right have they to the college crest, some fool will inquire?

Every right. They *are* the college.

* * *

It is most unfair to lump lodging-house keepers under college servants. They do not serve the colleges. Primarily they serve themselves. Yet many undergraduates have to leave their college—some after their first year if the college authorities do not like them—and spend their final years at the University in lodgings. It is generally more expensive to live in lodgings than the college. And lodgings may be anywhere. And landladies may be anything.

Some are admirable, great characters, not too prying, not too strict about hours, not too particular about their furniture, kind to you when you are ill, generous, humorous. I lodged in five different places at Oxford and two of my landladies were of this sort. But these good souls generally get into trouble with the authorities and are struck off the list.

What of the others? When I say that their rooms are expensive and often ugly, that they fawn to one's parents, and overcharge and aren't over-clean or are over-clean—when I say that they are just like the annual jokes about landladies that we read every holiday season, I have said enough.

'VARSITY TROPHIES OR FRESHMEN'S
FOLLIES

Chapter Five

THE APPROACHES TO OXFORD

Elsfield and Marston

The approaches to Oxford are the worst thing about it. None of them prepare you for a vision of the home of learning nestling grey among the elm surrounded meadows. I have made a mistake. There is *one* route, too circuitous and too laborious to be taken by any but the most romantic minded. You turn off the main road from High Wycombe just beyond Wheatley and make for Chipping Norton. After a few miles you branch left by shut-in lanes through grey Elsfield downhill to Marston. Here you take the footpath to Marston Ferry. At the ferry you board a punt or canoe or rob roy and paddle down the stream of the Cherwell to Magdalen Bridge.

The Cherwell is as romantic as it ever was—willows, meadows in which fritillaries have been found, a few boathouses and tea gardens with parents pouring out tea for self-conscious undergraduates. Under willows

97

you will see punts moored close into the bank. The intellectual head of an undergraduette appears above the cushions, the pipe smoke of her admirer winds up among the leaves. A gramophone plays a dance tune. Gradually the subtle variations of a Bach fugue break in upon the dance. A punt rounds the corner, full of clever looking men in grey flannel trousers and shirt sleeves—sleeves of what shirts setting off what Czechoslovakian peasant-art ties!—this probably contains one of the younger dons with some promising pupils. Soon they will all be off on a reading party to the Pyrenees and when they return very few of them will be on speaking terms.

CHERWELL'S BANKS

But let us not look into the future while we can see so much of the past.

As the shouts of the boys and the encouragement of the swimming instructors die away from the bathing place of the Dragon School behind us, the river takes a turn at a discreet female bathing place, and part of Oxford University is before us. We are in the University Parks where, of an afternoon, games are played on those dreary levels of sparse grass. In the distance Keble College pricks the skyline with its turrets and iron decorations. The river is spanned by an elegant concrete foot bridge, which humps itself like a Magpie Moth Caterpillar (*Abraxas grossulariata*). The effect is quite Japanese. This is the prettiest bridge for miles, a delicate piece of engineering unspoiled by "architectural" additions.

Hoarse shouts, splashes, and screams sound above the thunder of a weir. We are at Parson's Pleasure, the open-air bathing place. There may be many parsons there, for all we can tell—clergymen are a great feature of North Oxford—but everyone is naked. Bodies lie stretched on the grass, looking up between the poplars, pipes jammed into mouths, sunlight dappling bald or long-haired heads.

We pull the boat over the rollers and the Cherwell winds on through the meadows of Mesopotamia to Magdalen Bridge. A gravel walk follows the river. Earnest students walk briskly along it, airing their brains before an evening's study. Snatches of conversation float down to us—"Herodotus . . . first class mind . . . an alpha man . . . Aristotelian . . . Hegelian . . . Economic. . . . ." The conversation dies away. The river bends. The banks are steep and scooped away by the narrow stream. The trees of Addison's walk hang over us. We are shut in by mud and grass. Somewhere about here it is, that you can hear the bells of Oxford better than from anywhere else. The sound sifted from the motor traffic carries across the meadows. I cannot particularize the bend in the stream without going in a boat to show you. It is some yards from Magdalen Bridge for the roar of the main road traffic is scarcely audible. Then you have to be spared the blaring of portable gramophones. But there *is* such a bend and no time is better to hear the bells than shortly before six on a still summer evening.

One—two, *One*—two, *One*—two. New College Tower is calling to choral evensong. Elsewhere college chapels and little high church places of worship where a lonely vicar will run through evensong to an old lady from North Oxford, keep up an insistent tinkle. Then Magdalen Tower breaks into a chime quite near, one two three four, four three two one, one two three four, four three two one. This sets the bells going all over the town. Finally the heavy boom from Tom Tower, Christ Church strikes the hours and puts an end to the dispute. Now the bells start for evening chapel at Magdalen, and somewhere a church tower, probably Carfax, strikes a belated six to defy the thunderings of Tom.

An Oxford University Chest

People have noticed these bells across the Oxford rivers for years. At the end of the eighteenth century, Cowper's friend, the Reverend James Hurdis, Professor of Poetry, thus remarked them:

> So have I stood at eve on Isis' banks,
> To hear the merry Christ-church bells ring round.
> So have I sat too in thy honoured shades
> Distinguish'd Magdalen, on Cherwell's brink,
> To hear thy silver Wolsey tones so sweet.
> And so too have I paus'd and held my oar
> And suffer'd the slow stream to bear me home,
> No speed required while Wykeham's peal was up.

With a bump we knock into the cluster of boats round Magdalen

MAGDALEN COLLEGE FROM THE BRIDGE

100

Bridge, thread our way through cushioned empty punts shaded by Magdalen Tower. So by willows, lovers, intellectuals, boys, bathers, bells we have come right into the High Street of the University City; what more appropriate approach?

From London by Maidenhead, 58 Miles

First the Great Worst Road and then that battle-ground of country and industry which stretches to Slough and beyond. The victory has been to unplanned industry, wires strung across the sky in all directions hold the glaring, temporary fabric together. Bereted bounders roar past in rakish cars with cuties beside them, popping down to Maidenhead. Commercial gentlemen cut in and out in pretentious saloons, stacked high with samples in the back. Lorry upon lorry poisons the air and holds up the traffic. Maidenhead, home of night clubs and overworked angry policemen, has a beautiful bridge in the rich deep melancholy of the Thames Valley. An air of riches recently gained pervades the journey now to Henley and beyond.

The country recovers from the attack as we reach Benson. At Dorchester Abbey is the Jesse window more fascinating than beautiful and a grim-faced recumbent effigy, a moving piece of sculpture. Notice the tin Protestant Church in Dorchester erected because the Abbey was so High Church.

Nuneham Courtenay, neat village, a minor Milton Abbas. Georgian Church and palatial private Georgian House of Lord Harcourt are a mile from the village.

The City of learning is upon us. We straighten ourselves out of torpor and have a bet on who shall see the first dreaming spire. Dear traveller, there are no spires to see. Slough and Maidenhead are upon us again. This villa-strewn, red muddle is Littlemore, where, in 1842, Newman once retired to fast and pray and hide himself from Oxford's angry

Protestants and agnostics. And that large building like a workhouse is the lunatic asylum.

This next suburb with its garages, factories and villas is Iffley. Down by the river is the famous Norman church, so Norman in detail, so thoroughly restored, so enriched with zigzag and pellet moulding, as to make one doubt its authenticity.

As a foreground to our first view of the University are some arid playing fields on our left, like recreation grounds in Manchester. They remind us that Oxford is the home of sport as well as culture. That plain yellow stone church is the home of the Cowley Fathers. These little roads also like Manchester, to the right, contain the lodgings of struggling students who dream of getting a good enough degree to enable them to become secondary school teachers and so die happy on the Burnham scale. With these sad thoughts we come to Magdalen Bridge.

From London by High Wycombe, 54 Miles.

Out of London by Shepherds Bush and miles of trolley buses to Uxbridge, a town which still manages to keep its individuality despite the march of "progress". The houses of Metroland and beechy Bucks dot the landscape by Gerrards Cross, Quaker Jordans, Beaconsfield and on to Wycombe. The half timbered style is favoured and there is an atmosphere of riches, not quite so great nor quite so ostentatious, perhaps, as in the Thames Valley, until you get to High Wycombe.

The town is the seat of the chair industry (don's joke). The delicate colonnade supporting the Town Hall is worth seeing. Afterwards, on the Oxford Road, a straight and hideous mile has a mysterious and beautiful end, for rising up as a termination to the view is the sinister hill of West Wycombe whose church on the top has a gilded ball upon the tower. Cowper in his letters records the ghosts seen flitting about among the junipers on the slopes. Probably they were (and are) the ghosts of members of the "Monks of Medmenham and Knights of St. Francis", a collection of eighteenth century wits who practised black magic first at Medmenham on the Thames and later on Sir John Dashwood's estate at West Wycombe. Some members are buried in the strange flint and stone enclosure to the east of the church. If you look through the arches you will see niches on the inside walls which were to hold urns containing the ashes of the members. There was an urn in the middle of the enclosure to the memory of one of the wickedest of them all Paul Whitehead, a poet, who died in 1774.

The church is well worth seeing (the key may be had on enquiry in the village at the bottom of the hill). Psychic people are afraid to go into it. Certainly it has few of the trappings associated with a place of worship. The ceiling is a magnificent example of eighteenth century plaster work and is highly coloured. The chancel is low and dark and delicately decorated. The reading desks and font are strange rococco pieces. It has been remarked that they contain no symbols of the Christian religion among them. If you have the strength, climb up the tower into the swaying wooden ball outside it. From here you can see the rolling beech clad Chilterns and the well planted park of Sir John Dashwood's house at the foot of the hill by the village.

On your way down the hill you will notice a dark, flint entrance in the Gothic style of two hundred years ago. Yews screen it from the wind. A passage, leading for many yards into the heart of the hill, branches and discovers chambers and more passages.

The village of West Wycombe through which the road passes, is rescued from development, being now the property of the Society of Arts. It is a narrow street containing old houses in a variety of styles and a noble

Georgian Inn. To me the place still seems to remember the Hell Fire Club and to be unnaturally dark and still, taking little notice of the roaring traffic that goes through it day and night.

The road runs nobly on through the Chilterns, turns down a steep wooded hill and now you begin to feel you are near Oxford. There is no more chalk, many houses are built of stone, the grey villages stand down the lanes among elms. At the Brimpton Cross Roads you would do well to turn back along the Thame Road and branch off down a drive to Rycote Liberty. The mellow brick house, before a deserted reedy lake, is only a fragment of the former large house of the Earls of Abingdon. But the well disposed owners have the key to the grey stone church that stands on the slope above the lake. And it is the church which you must see, for this is one of the most remarkable buildings in England. Outside it looks no more than a simple country church. Within, it is decayed but palatial. An altar piece in the plain classic manner confronts you. There are a Jacobean screen and two enormous pews elaborately painted. One of the pews has an organ loft above it, the other has a domed roof painted wiht gold stars on the inside. The old pews remain in the nave, so do the west gallery and the marble pavement of the chancel.

The romantic name and natural surroundings of Rycote Liberty are not more lovely than the interior of the church, not even when the graveyard is white with snowdrops as I have often seen it.

There is nothing on the main road to detain you now till we get to Oxford. Near Wheatley you will notice some of the ugliest Council Houses in the country, built in the half timbered style alien to the neighbourhood, and set above the main road. Beyond Wheatley is the turning to Chipping Norton which I mentioned on page 97.

Headington which you next approach is a mass of untidy speculative buildings, blaring arcades of shops and finally a neat council house scheme. The village of old Headington has a church with a Norman chancel arch for the delight of antiquarians only.

To the South-East of Headington, there is indeed some semi-rural scenery, beyond the miles of allotments. The country becomes sandy and conifer ridden in the Aldershot style. But it is certainly pleasanter, though speculative building has done much of the work completed by the army at Aldershot. From Shotover Hill the view all round is unforgettable. I have been told by a don, but not the Professor of Geography, that if you look East there is nothing between you and the Ural Mountains. But then, as I told the don, the earth is round so there must be.

John Milton came to the village of Forest Hill near here for his wife and Milton's grandfather was ranger of the Shotover Woods. William Julius Mickle, a good eighteenth century poet, is buried in Forest Hill Churchyard (the church was spoiled by Sir Gilbert Scott). He wrote a fake antique poem about Cumnor Hall, a place on the other side of Oxford, the first lovely quatrain of which sticks in my memory:

> "The dews of Summer nighte did falle,
> The moone (sweete regente of the skye)
> Silver'd the walles of Cumnor Halle,
> And manye an oake that grewe therebye."

And as the dews of summer night fall, let us drive down Headington Hill where there are still trees and parkland. And here we sink into Oxford. Notice the decent old almshouses on your left as you approach Magdalen Bridge. The sun by now will be behind the towers and spires, making them a black silhouette, familiar on a thousand picture postcards, book covers, writing-paper heads. I prefer them with the sun setting on them and will go to the western side of Oxford.

But before we go, look back at Magdalen Bridge. There in the gathering dusk is the road from Maidenhead and Henley and behind us the road by which we came. Between the two runs the Cowley Road and the sky is read above it but not with sunset. The glow comes from the new town of East Oxford which has sprung up round the Morris works. Multiple stores, arcades, cinemas, neon lights, buses, a life of its own make East Oxford as big and important a town as this once mediaeval city we are about to enter. The famous battles of town and gown (town *v.* university) are not dead. They may not be carried on as they were in the past with staves and fists and arrows; the battle is done with bricks, red bricks. The red brick houses of the town have advanced right up to Magdalen Bridge, balked there by the meadows of the Cherwell they have encircled the town on other sides and crept right into the main streets of the University itself. Let us approach Oxford from the West and see the worst.

FOLLY BRIDGE AND THE BARGES

OXFORD FROM THE WEST

Swindon 30 miles—Fairford 28 miles—Bristol 76 miles.

And now we come down Cumnor Hill. What an approach to the city of learning! What learned architecture! Here the half timbered villa holds its own boldly beside the bogus-modern, here the bay windows and stained glass front door survey the niggling rock garden and arid crazy paving. Those slopes which the Scholar Gipsy haunted are now dotted with residences raised piecemeal and looking like so many slices of cake. Only Wytham woods on the opposite hill retain an uninvaded calm. The Scholar Gipsy must wash his bronzed face in birdbaths and sleep under the shade of stone toadstools if he is still to roam the slopes of Cumnor Hill. Do you think he has gone to the Hinkseys, those grey stone villages with their twisted stacks that Thyrsis knew? A byepass, rarely used, cuts through the favourite fields. Down here by the main road is a row of red villas with stone dressings worthy of Luton herself or something of which even the Great West Road might be proud.

True between the Hinkseys, (new strung with poles and wire and encircled by villas) and the City of learning lies a marsh so flat, so wet and so unpleasant that only its edges have been approached by progress.

One turning this Scholar Gipsy might undertake if he still tries to see Oxford as it once was. The open lane to Wytham still skirts the woods, and the meadows stretch with their willows to the Isis, without the bricks of progress. Wytham Village is still grey and covered with creepers. The churchyard with its little door looking through to the peacock-trodden lawns of Wytham Manor, is still dank and dark and green like some pre-Raphaelite picture. Better still that lane with its gates, crosses the meadow to Godstow, and, as you reach the Isis, there are the ruins of Godstow and there is the Trout Inn. The weir still roars so that you cannot hear yourself speak and some miles upstream the Evenlode joins the Isis unmolested, among meadows where I have still found bird's nest orchis and fritillaries.

But once beyond the Trout and the horror begins again towards Wolvercote and the paper mills. Once that village used to be pleasantly ugly with its white brick villas looking more like a suburb of Cambridge than of Oxford and with the railway hooting about all round. Now enterprise has erected a broad avenue of villas, many of them indeed with grey green roofs and light walls, so that the general air of a rubbish heap has gone and we are back in Luton or Golder's Green. Wytham behind us seems in another planet.

OXFORD FROM THE NORTH

The roads converge at St. Giles: from the Cotswolds, the yellow-grey stone walls, the high damp-looking manors, the big bare fields, the beech clumps, the deep valleys, Morris curtains fluttering from stone cottage windows, yew hedges and delphiniums, the upper reaches of the Evenlode:

The Approaches to Oxford

"The tender Evenlode that makes
    Her meadows hush to hear the sound
Of waters mingling in the brakes,
    And binds my heart to English ground."

(Belloc.)

Tea places run by gentlefolk, stone toadstools, stonecrop, a few large parks and houses, hardly any bad speculative building, all this and more to the north-west; from Banbury and the Midlands, the brown stone of North Oxfordshire, less flaky than the yellow-grey of the Cotswolds' great spires:

> King's Sutton for length
> Adderbury for strength,
> Bloxham for beauty:

a good many nasty little red brick pretentiousnesses spoiling the brown villages, excessive telegraph wires, an unpleasant feeling that Birmingham is not far off, petrol stations, main roads, one or two hidden places that are better than anywhere, all this and more to the north; Grey Bicester, "Bicestershire", the smart hunting district, special train to London in the mornings, hearty after hunting breakfast, first-class passengers, first-class fences, foxes in every covert, rain always, the long sinister flats of Otmoor, willows, elms and poplars, greystone houses, the bits of Bucks that look like Oxon and the bits of Oxon that look like Warwicks; efficient small houses with hot baths for tired hunting people, plenty of hot water and electric light, uncared for gardens and tidy stables, twisty lanes and the fearful devastation of the jerry builder at Kidlington, these to the north-east.

The roads converge in St. Giles embracing North Oxford with long arms. North Oxford deserves a section to itself and shall have it.

At present I can only spot a few places beyond North Oxford which are worth a visit.

Woodstock. Many Georgian and earlier houses, mostly stone. Stupid arrangement of electric light poles ruins the whole town. Blenheim, seat of the Duke of Marlborough, should be seen. The detail is imposing, the general effect surprising. Certainly nowhere in England, probably nowhere in the world, is such an overpowering illusion of grandeur produced by the skilful planting of trees as in this park. The full beauty of it bursts on the view as you enter from the town gateway. The lake, winding perhaps for ever, the beeches billowing down to it, the great beech trunks in the foreground, the wide skyscape bathed with leaves on the right of the picture. The great bridge binding the whole design together. Vanbrugh was never better than here. Capability Brown never more inspired. No wonder English landscape gardening was famous all over the world. (You will notice that the new plantations of trees show less inspiration and will spoil everything when they attain majority.) No age but the eighteenth century in England so perfectly understood the natural beauties of its countryside, nor conceived the planting of it in such extensive sweeps, such ample speculations. Woodstock Park is open to the public. The Palace is not. The gardens sometimes are.

Ditchley is a superb Renaissance house. Only a few years ago, before the sale after the death of the late Lord Dillon, it contained one of the best collections of furniture and paintings in the country.

Great Tew is a picturesque brown stone and thatched village among trees and greens and box hedges. It has the melancholy of a late Victorian water colour and was laid out by J. C. Loudon (1783–1843), the landscape gardener.

Rousham has a garden laid out by Kent with numerous avenues and temples. An interesting example (though a private one) of the transition from the seventeenth century formal garden to the wide romantic landscape treatment of Blenheim Park.

Yarnton should be seen on your way back down the Woodstock Road. The grey old manor rises above pollarded limes. The church has much pretty old glass and a chapel in a seventeenth century Perpendicular style, rich with the monuments of the Spencer family from the tarnished blue and red and gold of the seventeenth century, through the English grey and veined Baroque to the severity of the white Greek Revival with its neatly arranged inscriptions.

Charlton-on-Otmoor should be seen by those who bother to turn off the twisty Bicester Road. The sullen presence of Otmoor, that unexpected fen, broods over this damp, alarming district. The village is grey and comparatively treeless as are most Otmoor villages. The church has an elaborate late-mediaeval screen surmounted by an evergreen cross, pagan-looking despite its Christian symbolism.

The best country remains, however, to the west. Cross the stripling Thames at Bablockhythe, trying to forget the modernistical public house, and the bungalows, and see Northmoor and Stanton Harcourt. Do not take your stinking motor-car. Use footpaths. Walk by high hedges and heavy elms and melancholy stretches of water. You will still find in the parts I have mentioned near Oxford which have escaped development, a lush country wherein, at any moment, you might meet Matthew Arnold, or over whose marshes you might come on a group of undergraduates helping Ruskin to build a road. The best contemporary description of Oxfordshire is to be found in John Piper's *Oxon* (Shell Guides).

One village, almost in Oxford, remains for me to describe. Among the villas beyond the stations, off the Western approach to Oxford, is a turning to the North called Binsey Lane. Once over the humped iron bridge and you are in the country again among the willows and meadows. Binsey is still unspoiled and its prospect of Port Meadow viewed from its yellow public house, is the best view of Oxford to be had from the West. Further down the lane is the little church, and a once famous holy well beside it. Here a ritual has been devised. Drop a small stone into the well and ask yourself a question. Walk into the church without saying anything and open the Bible on the lectern. The first verse you see will give the answer to your question.

Wytham and Binsey are the less hackneyed of Oxford's lost causes on the edge of Oxford. I have a fear that they will not be lost much longer.

ARCHITECTURAL TOUR

Tour of Buildings.

Everything in and about the University is near enough to everything else to justify my giving you an alphabetical order of things to see.

ADDISON'S WALK. *See* MAGDALEN COLLEGE.

ST. ALDATES is the name of the road going down to Folly Bridge from Carfax. It is also the name of an Evangelical church by Pembroke College. The church has been so "restored" that it is indistinguishable from a Victorian one.

ALL SAINTS CHURCH floats like a galleon above the Carfax end of the High. It was built in the Renaissance style, 1706–8, by Dean Aldrich who doubtless intended it as a termination to a vista to be seen from Trinity College Chapel as well as the unused entrance gates on the Broad. Unluckily the Gothic façades of Jesus, Exeter and Lincoln, the three colleges in the Turl get in the way. All Saints Church stands as the last good building in the eastern end of High Street. Towards Carfax good architecture is obliterated by modern commercial renaissance and Jacobethan, and the surviving upper stories of eighteenth century work and earlier which you may see from the top of a 'bus, are mostly covered by signs.

The tower is one of the most successful compositions in Oxford, its steeple sitting gracefully upon it, not as a separate object stuck on afterwards, but seeming to be a natural culmination to the tower itself.

All Saints is called The City Church, because the Mayor and Corporation are supposed to use it. Its services are broad to low. The interior of the church seems indeed to be like one of the City churches of London. There, is the wrought iron work, there, the sculptured decoration, the solid woodwork and handsome organ case, the smell of well-cared-for hassocks, the atmosphere of merchant wealth. The inside is spacious and singularly well proportioned. Even when we consider that the pews have been cut down, the arrangements at the east end altered and a good view of the delicate stone work and modelled ceiling impeded by repulsive Victorian glass in what was considered to be a Renaissance manner in the latter half of that century, we still must admire the interior. Notice the altar piece and pulpit. Shakespeare stood godfather to Sir William Davenant, at the font here.

Dean Aldrich designed Peckwater Quad, the Fellows' Buildings at Corpus, as well as this church. He was an amateur architect as were so many of the greater architects of his time.

All Souls College.

BUILDINGS. The front presents a diversity of styles, the most outstanding part of which is the eighteenth century Warden's Lodgings,* a private House at the Queen's College end of the front. The public enters

the college under a carving of Souls in Purgatory. The small mediaeval quad which you first see is undistinguished, yet it is worth your while proceeding to the chapel, dull and over-restored as this building looks from without. The entrance passage with its umbrella stand and holy water stoup has pretty mid-fifteenth century fan vaulting.

Your first impression of the chapel is the best. Much fifteenth century glass, the spacious antechapel (diminutive if you have already seen New College Chapel which is on the same T-shaped plan) and dominating the whole view a gigantic classical screen (attributed, on what evidence I do not know, to Sir Christopher Wren) painted in dark colours which throws

* Probably designed originally by Dr. George Clarke (1661-1736).

it up to perfection against the white stonework. Originally an altar piece by Sir James Thornhill (1675–1734) set off the screen at the East End. Unfortunately the remains of a reredos were discovered in the last century and £10,000 was spent in removing Sir James' work and filling up the reredos with comical statuary. Many windows were filled with horrible glass and a transparency by Francis Eginton (1737–1805) was removed. How the screen came to be spared passes comprehension. The stalls are partly original.

The surprises All Souls has in store yet await you. It is characteristic of Oxford that the approaches to its grandest sights are mean and difficult to find. If, on leaving the chapel, you turn up a passage to the east of it, you will come into one of Oxford's best quadrangles. Look to your left and there, above a colonnade rises the Radcliffe Camera, ahead of you is the huge Codrington library (Dr. George Clarke and Sir Nathaniel Lloyd, 1669–1745), to your right the celebrated twin towers of All Souls. These towers were designed by Nicholas Hawksmoor (1661–1736). They are, like his twin towers to Westminster Abbey, an essay in the Gothic style. They are designed for shadows and, like the whole quad, look their best when the sun or moon is in the south. You will then notice the insistence on vertical lines given by the huge buttresses round the quad and emphasized by the towers. A serious proposal was made, a year or two ago, to remove Hawksmoor's twin towers at All Souls. At any time but the present, such cocksure vandalism would have been unbelievable.

Walk down the colonnade on your left, noticing the ironwork of the entrance gates centring on the Radcliffe Camera, till you reach the small door, another undistin-

Orrery in the Bodleian.

Brasenose College from the Radcliffe.

guished approach, which leads to the room which leads to the great Codrington Library. This building, so Gothickal without, is Renaissance within. Its length is subtly graded to its height and it just avoids being a passage. The huge plain circular headed windows down one side make one wish that the temptation to stained glass had been avoided, as it has been here, in other classic buildings of Oxford. [The Hawksmoor dining hall at All Souls is spoiled by modern glass.] Notice the bookcases and the painted woodwork, a proof, if any was wanted, that wooden fittings are better not pickled: notice the pilasters of alternate Doric and Ionic up the bookcases. Notice too the busts and statuary, a remarkable collection.

There are three details to notice on your way out. (1) The elaborate sundial, designed by Sir Christopher Wren, among the pinnacles of the large quad. (2) The oval stone buttery with its classic vaulting designed by Dr. George Clarke. (3) The chimney piece of gray marble in the dining hall and the Thornhill portraits.

P E O P L E. There are now no undergraduates at All Souls. Every member is a fellow and a graduate (excepting the college servants). "Well-born, well-dressed and moderately educated" was once the usual description of a Fellow of All Souls. University Reform in the last hundred years has altered the title. A Fellowship at All Souls is now one of the greatest honours the University can bestow, it is the equivalent (and in the opinion of the Fellows, more than the equivalent) of being a Fellow of Kings at Cambridge, it entitles the recipient to the centre page should he send a letter to *The Times*,* it absolves him from unnecessary

truck with undergraduates: safe in the knowledge that he is surrounded by nothing but first-class brains, the All Souls Fellow may devote himself with passion to that research to which the University has called him.

Francis Gribble,* writing in 1910, says: "The unmannerly bookworm has never been wanted at All Souls. The scholar who is also a gentleman has always been preferred to him; and from the time of Sir Christopher Wren to the time of Lord Curzon of Kedleston, the college has generally been able to boast of some Fellow of wide fame, not of a rigidly academic character." A well-known Fellow of All Souls at the moment is Sir Charles Oman.

Besides Sir Christopher Wren (see Wadham College), Dr. George Clarke, Sir Nathaniel Lloyd, and Lord Curzon, the following were Fellows of All Souls:

Thomas Linacre (1460?–1524), Physician and classical scholar.

Thomas Sydenham (1624–1689), Physician.

Jeremy Taylor (1613–1667), Divine. Author of *Holy Living and Dying*, &c.

Sir William Blackstone (1723–1780). great lawyer and lesser poet.

Dr. Edward Young (1683–1765), Poet. *Night Thoughts*.

Philip, Duke of Wharton (1698–1731). Art connoisseur, racing man, President of Hell Fire Club, amateur architect, Royalist.

On January 14th each year a song is sung at gaudies about a mallard or duck which was said to have started out of a drain when the college was founded. Once a century the Fellows make a torchlight procession by night over the roofs of the college. The words of the song are seventeenth century

* *The Times* is sometimes called the *All Souls Parish Magazine*.

* *The Romance of Oxford Colleges*. Mills and Boon.

and are sung with great gusto by the older fellows.

ST. ALOYSIUS is the Roman Catholic Church opposite the west end of the church at the far end of St. Giles'. It was opened in 1873 by Cardinal Manning. The interior surpasses the exterior. The architect was Joseph Hansom who invented the Hansom cab.

ST. ANDREWS. A Norman Revival (1906–7) Evangelical Church in the Anglo-Jackson part of North Oxford. Hard greenish exterior, pale sticky interior.

ASHMOLEAN MUSEUM. This handsome building on the corner of Beaumont Street proclaims, opposite the Randolph Hotel, the virtues of the Classic Revival against the Gothic. It is the work of a scholarly architect, Professor C. R. Cockerell, who made the conjectural restoration of Halicarnassus and whose best work is the Sun Fire Office in the City of London. The Ashmolean—originally called Sir Robert Taylor's Institution and the University Galleries, really comprises an art gallery, a museum and the Taylorian Institute, headquarters of the Modern Languages Faculty. The whole block, called for convenience "The Ashmolean", was building 1841–8.

The last block Cockerell built, The Taylorian on the corner of St. Giles and Beaumont Street, is the best. Notice its proportions, its details and statuary. On all accounts, if you can get permission, take a look at the library inside, a most handsome late classic room. I think it is fair to say that the screen joining the Taylorians with its twin fortress down Beaumont Street, is too shallow and flat and the central

portico in this screen too diminutive for the noble blocks on either side. Despite these faults, the Ashmolean is the best nineteenth century building in Oxford and next to Queen's College and the Radcliffe Camera the best large classic building in the city. It is a better argument for the Romano-Greek Revival than Keble is for the Decorated, for it has beauty not only of proportion like Keble, but also of texture.

Tacked on to the Taylorian in a clumsy manner by a curved consol, of the wrong material, in the wrong place and with the wrong lines is an addition in a style which apes the Cockerell's fine Taylorian.

The Ashmolean is certainly worth visiting for the art gallery which is one of the best small collections in the world. Notice the Italians, the pre-Raphaelite and the English water colours. The museum part is more archaeological than interesting and is composed partly of the collections moved from the Old Ashmolean (q.v.) in Broad Street. The museum part of the Ashmolean is unwelcoming in the true museum tradition. Some people get as far as "Alfred's Jewel" and "Guy Fawkes' Lantern".

THE OLD ASHMOLEAN is a late seventeenth century wedge in between the Sheldonian and Exeter College in Broad Street. It was built to contain the curiosities of Elias Ashmole presented to Oxford in 1682. Such objects as "A corn two inches long, taken off a Toe of one Sarney a Wheelwright, of St. Aldate's Parish in Oxford, 1655" and "The Dodar-Birds, one of which watches whilst the other stoops down to drink" have disappeared and one has only to visit the arid antiquarian galleries of the New Ashmolean (*vide supra*) to realize that modern specialization would not tolerate such side-tracks, for it is to here that Elias

Ashmole's collection, or rather what remained of it, was removed. Thus Oxford lost some of the first museum in England.

Forget the insolence of Sir Gilbert Scott's Broad Street front of Exeter College and turn down by the side of the Sheldonian to examine the entrance doorway to the Old Ashmolean. This delicate work is ascribed (wrongly) to Wren. Though a little large for the manor-like building on to which it is tacked, it is a miracle of proportion in itself.

The upstairs part of the museum is crowded with orreries, celestial globes, astrolabes, sextants, theodolites, early microscopes, portable sundials, presided over by a portrait of the extinct Dodo bird burned by the order of the Vice-Chancellor in 1755. This collection is some compensation for the annihilation of Ashmole's curiosities, for the instruments are of rare beauty and intricacy and happily arranged.

In the rooms below, slip by slip, the Oxford Dictionary ploughed through the alphabet. Many a cultivated lexicographer and harassed messenger hurried in and out from down below, while the orreries brooded impassive and little visited over their heads.

Balliol College.

BUILDINGS. From no point external or internal, does Balliol appear a handsome conglomeration. Like a great battleship, the

Gothic buildings by Alfred Waterhouse sail along Broad Street. They were built in the late 1860's. On the corner of Broad Street

Keene's Fisher Building (1769) asserts a little distinction, while George Basevi's early nineteenth century block which continues down opposite St. Mary Magdalen's Church has been spoiled by the addition of a story of bed-sitters. On towards St. John's the buildings are correct but uninteresting revived Gothic, mostly this century.

Within, the college presents an untidy appearance and one can at least be grateful for the presence of trees and grass, for the old Dining Hall (1432) and the Library (1432–80).

Butterfield's chapel (1856–7) was a noble building and one of the best monuments to the "original" era of the Gothic Revival that Oxford possessed. Unluckily it has recently been done up in a new chaste manner of which Butterfield could hardly have approved and which has robbed it of the strong character it had. Notice the sixteenth century glass by Van Linge the younger.

The hall (1877) in the Garden Quad, by Waterhouse, is handsome outside.

Those who want to compare the odd, should notice the excellent proportions of the roof of Butterfield's chapel in relation to the walls supporting it. Though this building does not attempt to harmonize with its surroundings, it is an honest expression of its age. Now compare the awkward pitch of Waterhouse's roof to the hall and his even more disastrous arrangement of the upper stories of his Broad Street work.

PEOPLE. "It is fitting that Balliol 'the most progressive of our colleges' should have so large a proportion of its buildings modern." Thus wrote Dr. Wells in his *Oxford and its Colleges* (1st Edition, 1897), and in those days progress was still believed in. Balliol has done much to foster belief in the progress myth. It started as an obscure place with Scottish connections in about 1265. It remained obscure until the nineteenth century, despite the appearance of Adam Smith as an undergraduate in the 1740's. The Masters of Balliol found themselves saddled with Scottish undergraduates who came up as "Snell Exhibitioners", athirst for knowledge, abstemious and covenant-keeping. The Scots were given bad rooms and not encouraged. For one glorious moment in the eighteenth century, the master thought he had got rid of them to Hertford College which was then starting on "progressive" lines, under Richard Newton, the first university reformer. But the attempt failed. Had it not done so, Hertford not Balliol, would have been the place of brain boxes.

The rise of Balliol started with the mastership (1798–1819) of John Parsons. Parsons was a pioneer of the examination system and founded the Honours Schools in collaboration with Dr. Everleigh, Provost of Oriel, and Cyril Jackson, Dean of Christ Church.

Dr. Jenkyns succeeded him and reigned until 1842. He invented the idea of open scholarships. He engaged clever tutors. The old name of Balliol as a dear, dim, drinking college, was dead. Dr. Jenkyns was master when Blayds (C. S. Calverley) was up. There is an old chestnut, still repeated by guides, about Blayds and Dr. Jenkyns. Blayds was showing some ladies round Balliol. "That is the Master of Balliol's window", he said. Then he picked up a stone and threw it, smashing the glass. An angry face appeared. "And that is the Master of Balliol."

People writing of Jenkyns at the beginning of this century, find it hard to know how he managed to be so "great" a man. Stories about him mostly make him ridiculous.

So for us, it is hard to discover why Dr. Jowett* who succeeded him (1870–93) was so universally respected. Stories about him show him as rude. I have mentioned one already in chapter III. Here is another from Anthony Hope's *Memories and Notes*:

"J. Good morning.

A.H. Good morning, sir. May I go to London to eat my dinners on Saturday?

J. Yes.

A.H. May I stay over Monday night? My sister is to be married on Tuesday.

J. Yes.

A.H. And we have a family party on Tuesday evening. May I stay over that night?

J. No. Good morning,"

and I would advise those who want to read what seems a fair, not too grovelling, account of Jowett to seek it in Anthony Hope's book. In the true Balliol tradition of making education difficult and democratic, Jowett advocated a cheap university career, secondary education and university extension.

Edward Caird, one of those once-dreaded Snell Exhibitioners, succeeded Jowett and was a supporter of women's education and Oxford education for working men.

Dr. Strachan Davidson, who succeeded him, was one of the last gentlemanly, rather eccentric, and highly scholarly dons. He kept up the learned reputations of the college with a charming air of absent-mindedness.

After him was the famous A. L. Smith.

The present Master is a notable Socialist and Scot, and it is true to say that Balliol still governs the policy of Oxford University education as it always has done since alpha

---

*Between Jenkyns and Jowett comes Robert Scott, a more secondary figure, like his name which comes after Liddell's on the Lexicon.

The Cherwell.

and beta and gamma, raised or condemned a man for ever.

How deeply Balliol has eaten into the hearts of her sons we may discover when we find even Mr. Belloc singing:

Balliol made me, Balliol fed me,
    Whatever I had she gave me again;
And the best of Balliol loved and led me,
    God be with you, Balliol men.

That is writ across the heart probably even of Mr. Aldous Huxley, who has so accurately caught the Balliol atmosphere in his novels.

Regard this list of Balliol alumni, notice how disproportionately large is the nineteenth century section. Some of the men here moved to Fellowships elsewhere.

John Wycliffe, Master c. 1360.
William Grey (Bishop of Ely), d. 1478.
John Evelyn, 1620–1706.
Adam Smith, 1723–1790.
Sir William Hamilton, 1788–1856.
J. G. Lockhart, 1794–1854.
Robert Southey, 1774–1843.
Arthur Hugh Clough, 1819–1861.
Matthew Arnold, 1822–1888.
C. S. Calverley, 1831–1884.
A. C. Swinburne, 1837–1909.
Andrew Lang, 1844–1912.
John Addington Symonds, 1840–1893.
Archbishop Tait, 1811–1882.
Archbishop Temple, 1821–1902.
Cardinal Manning, 1808–1892.
W. G. Ward, 1812–1882.
Bishop Gore, 1853–1932.
Canon Scott Holland, 1847–1918.
Arnold Toynbee, 1852–1883.
Dean Stanley, 1815–1881.
Sir J. D. Coleridge, 1820–1894.
Sir William Anson, 1843–1914.
T. H. Green, 1836–1882.
Anthony Hope Hawkins, 1863–1934.

Canon Beeching, 1859–1919.
Lord Oxford and Asquith, 1852–1928.
Lord Peel, 1829–1912.
Lord Milner, 1854–1925.
Lord Curzon, 1859–1925.
H. Belloc, 1870–
Aldous Huxley, 1894–

This is only a selection. I have omitted Robert Browning, who was elected an honorary fellow, and therefore hardly counts. Even disregarding this omission, the list explains why Balliol is severely criticized by those who were not at it.

St. Barnabas Church is in "Jericho". "Thou hast a base and brickish skirt there" (G. M. Hopkins). Jericho is a criss-cross pattern of two-storied red brick streets, for the most part broad, unadorned, mercifully, by bow windows, and rapidly being "cleared" by the progressive local council, in favour of other two-storied houses far further out. It is an early industrial settlement in Oxford, connected vaguely with the University Press and various small industries. The inhabitants are not scouts, rather one might say scouts of scouts—and all the more human for that. The streets pour down from Walton Street to the railway.

The slender campanile of St. Barnabas Church, dominates Jericho and it is a nice experience on a Sunday morning to hear the tubular bells call over the housetops, to see the unperturbed Jericho-dwellers polishing up a knocker and the many students of liturgiology walking down Cardigan Street from the University. Not that St. Barnabas does nothing for the parish: it has the most live and active social organization of all Oxford churches: but high mass at 11 on Sunday is an Oxford "sight" and the University, on that day in the week, still

Christchurch Cathedral.

comes to St. Barnabas as it did, in greater numbers, when this was a pioneer church of the Catholic Revival.

The building is in the Lombardic style and must have looked better when its brick exterior was clean and it stood Guardi-like above the Oxford Canal (see photograph by entrance). It was opened in 1869. The architect was Sir A. Blomfield and I have no hesitation in saying St. Barnabas is far the best of his work I have seen—and I have seen much.

The unfortunate internal decorations put in 1893 have been partially removed. The church now stands out as by far the best Victorian church in Oxford.

BISHOP KING'S PALACE. A genuine half-timbered, gabled building off St. Aldate's with the arms of Edward VI on it. Several of the houses here have fine plaster ceilings of the date, notably a little pull-in tea place next door to the greengrocer's. The palace contains a Roman Catholic Chapel, unexpected behind the arms of the little Protestant Prince.

BLACKFRIARS is an undistinguished building alongside Pusey House in St. Giles. It belongs to the Dominicans and produces an excellent magazine. The chapel is flat and spacious, but not effective.

BLENHEIM. That undergraduate or visitor lacks sense who does not at once go to Woodstock and enter the park at Blenheim from the town. Once through Sir William Chambers' archway and he will be confronted by the finest piece of landscape gardening in Britain. An islanded weed-covered lake curving under a massive bridge (by Vanbrugh) to further possibly vaster lakes, edged with beech trees. The palace

to the left, an uneven train of Baroque projections by swelling grass banks. Park laid out by eighteenth century Capability Brown. Palace (not open to public) by Vanbrugh. I mention this place twice in the book to draw attention to it.

BOAR'S HILL. What undergraduate has not pushed his bicycle up or ditched his car among the sandy, house-encumbered lanes of Boar's Hill? Shortly before the war when North Oxford was thought rather stuffy and Victorian, when taste was veering from the Gothic to the Garden City, from the high church to the Quaker, from the pink may, laburnum and lace curtain to chintzes and ever-open windows, when conifers and Frilford were considered pretty, the wandering married dons moved to the heights of Boar's Hill, a sandy tract of fir-planted Berkshire country. The increase in motor traffic has filled up the gaps between the greater houses, with smaller, and now all the world has tea among the pine trees in many an architect-designed abode.

Many of the literary lights of this hill are out, or shining away in the Cotswolds. In its heigh-day, Boar's Hill was a country centre, especially during Sunday tea-time, of University intellect. Dr. Bridges, the late Laureate, would talk to a select band in his ample drawing room, John Masefield would produce plays, Lady Keeble would recite Shakespeare, Miss Jackson would give musical parties. Sir Arthur Evans almost alone holds the fort, surrounded by conifers in several acres of ground.

BODLEIAN LIBRARY. The stairs lead visitors to the jewel-like centre of this library. The late Mr. Falconer Madan, once Bodley's librarian, says that it ranks

Between Tom Quad and Peckwater, Christchurch.

Tom Quad, Christ Church. The tower on the right is known as "the meat safe". The shadow of Tom Tower is to be seen.

about eighth in the great libraries of the world, and first in university libraries. The Radcliffe Camera is almost entirely taken up with its catalogue. Passages underground are lined with its books and will continue so to be lined even with Sir Giles Gilbert Scott's structure on the corner of Broad Street.

The original library was made by Humphrey Duke of Gloucester, an educated son of Henry IV. Edward VI's Commissioners destroyed this in 1550 and only three of Duke Humphrey's manuscripts have come back to the library.

Sir Thomas Bodley started a university library again in 1598 and it was opened in 1602 with 2,000 volumes. It grew to its present labyrinthine extent because Sir Thomas Bodley "made an agreement with the Stationery Company—an agreement confirmed by all Copyright Acts of later times—by which one copy of every book published by licensed printers and publishers in Great Britain was to be sent to the library".* I cannot discover whether *The Happy Mag*, *Rainbow*, *London Life*, and *Sexton Blake* are in the Bodleian, because I do not know what the authorities define as a book. Anyhow there are about 13,000,000 volumes there at present.

The valuable books it contains, the autographs, illuminated manuscripts, paintings, relics, &c., are too numerous to mention. But while you study these in the cases I would beg you to remember that the rules of the library are very strict. No smoking. No drinking. No speaking. Only thinking. If you so much as creak a board, some angry, bespectacled face will crane at you from a horsebox. If you hold a camera in your hand, cupid will snatch it. Even kings are subject to Bodley's thrall. No book may be

* Rice-Oxley, *Oxford Renowned.*

taken away. Charles I tried it on and was refused. Cromwell too was foiled.

BOTANIC GARDEN. Of a summer afternoon when the splash of punt poles is heard on the Cherwell, and the High Street traffic is deadened by the intervening architecture, and as Magdalen Tower, looking its best, strikes the quarters, I recommend a walk in the Botanic Garden. Those who know Rowlandson's delicately coloured landscape *The Gardener's Offering* will find in Oxford's Botanic Garden the same wealth of carefully planted trees, beds in various subdued hues of green, the straight walks and unspectacular plants, the sense of a mellow enclosing wall, and the air of well-kept desertion, noticeable in that picture. In the 'nineties, the garden was extended beyond its west wall to the Cherwell Banks where are some greenhouses. In one of them is a sensitive plant which you are not allowed to touch, but which is well worth touching.

The Baroque entrance gate is by Nicholas Stone (1586–1647), monumental sculptor. The second quadrangle in St. John's College may be his work, too. The garden was founded in 1621. There is an excellent late Georgian building at the Cherwell end of the block, designed in 1835 by H. J. Underwood who built St. Paul's Church in Walton Street.

Brasenose College.

BUILDINGS. That building of somewhat municipal appearance, with elaborate Gothic bow windows overhanging the ground floor and a gabled roof brought to a halt by a square tower—all in public library Perpendicular—that building between All Saints and St. Mary's in the High, is part of Brasenose College. It was designed by the ubiquitous Sir Thomas Jackson (1887 and 1910), a man of great culture, who wrote better than he practised.

The principal entrance to the college is in Radcliffe Square. Here a tower entrance gives on to an early sixteenth century quadrangle of the usual type—black and patched

grey stone up two storeys, small hooded windows, ancient dining hall on the left, chapel and library at right angles to it.

The distinguishing feature of this otherwise dull quadrangle is the third storey row of gables, an Early Jacobean survival which makes one visualize what the quads of New College, Jesus, Pembroke, Corpus, St. John's, and others were like before the upper storeys were neatly finished off in the eighteenth or nineteenth centuries. The feathery many-planed quality of this uneven arrangement of roofs is best appreciated from the roof of the Radcliffe Camera. To the centre quadrangle a statue of two men fighting was presented by Dr. Clarke in 1727 and removed in 1881.

The hall is worth seeing, as the last one, to give up the mediaeval system of having a large fire in the middle and letting the smoke and fumes go out through a hole in the roof (now surmounted by a lantern).

The library is a small handsome building within, re-modelled in the earlier manner of James Wyatt, when he was influenced by the Adam style. In the library are the elevations designed by Sir John Soane for the High

Street front of the college. Would that they had been carried out! We would then have had examples of all the great days of English architecture in the High Street, instead of a plethora of revived Gothic and Jacobean. His design was in the Greek manner, severe and somewhat reminiscent of his work along the principal front of the Bank of England.

The chapel is interesting to architectural students because it shows the struggle between Classic and Gothic—a fan tracery ceiling, Gothic windows (in the eyes of some writers "debased") and classical fittings— few of which have survived a vigorous re-Renaissancing by Kempe and others, so that the building now presents little appearance of antiquity. An interesting east window of enamelled glass by Pearson (late eighteenth century) was removed to the west end where it is not seen to advantage.

If you leave Brasenose by the Radcliffe Square entrance, take the first turn to the left and look up at those windows opposite the high wall of the Fellows' Garden of Exeter. From one of these the devil on horseback pulled out the black soul of an undergraduate and charged away with it into the night. This was in the days of the Brasenose Hell Fire Club (1828–1834). Even now psychic people say they have heard horse's hoofs bearing down upon them in that lane at night; have thought they must be ridden down and then unaccountably escaped, for the ghost now is only a ghost of sound.

PEOPLE. Every guide book will give you reasons for the curious name of this college: many tell you that it is called colloquially B.N.C.: others point out that the men of Brasenose Hall migrated to Stamford in Lincs. in 1334 and were driven back to Oxford by Royal command (no Oxford

M.A. was allowed to lecture in Stamford until 1827): others remark that the undergraduates of Brasenose were liable to corporal punishment under the Foundation Statutes. They might be birched for "speaking English in public."

The list of distinguished men at this college will show you that its great days were in the early nineteenth century, when Oxford glowed purple and grey among green fields like the aquatints which illustrate it.

Great men visited Brasenose, the greatest architect of the day—Sir John Soane—was called in by Brasenose only, of all Oxford colleges; the Hell Fire Club flourished: the Phoenix Wine Club was the most important dining club in Oxford: during these days Frodsham Hodson was Principal (1809–1822), who drove the last stage into Oxford with post horses "lest it should be said that 'the first Tutor of the first College of the First University of the world entered it with a pair'."*

What Balliol is to Oxford University now, Brasenose was then. It was the leading college. But it led to a different Oxford and reflected the Oxford it led. Verdant Green calls the Brasenose men "a very gentlemanly set" and so they were throughout the nineteenth century.

Of course, by the beginning of the nineteenth century one of the connotations of gentlemanliness was a love of sport. Part of the new Brasenose tradition was sportsmanship. The churchmanship of Brasenose was of a muscular variety. Dean Hole, whose Reminiscences are well worth reading for their light into the character of a jolly, breezy, not too intellectual padre, was at Brasenose. The Rev. R. H. Barham, author of *Ingoldsby Legends*, another jolly clergyman, was also there. It is of him that the

* *Memoirs*, Mark Pattison.

well-known story is told, just as it has been told of other people.

Tutor: Why are you often absent from chapel?

Barham: The fact is, sir, you are too late for me.

Tutor: Too late?

Barham: Yes, sir. I cannot sit up till seven o'clock in the morning; I am a man of regular habits, and unless I get to bed by four or five at latest, I am really fit for nothing next day."

Bishop Heber (who found the food bad when he was an undergraduate four years before Hodson was Principal) and his elder brother, Richard Heber, who collected more books than anyone else in the world has done, were also at Brasenose.

The last distinguished literary man to be at Brasenose was Walter Pater. He came as a Fellow from Queen's. By the time he was there, the college had attained the reputation for muscular activity which was incipient during the centuries and has now burst out into a scholarship for proficiency at Rugby football. So far as we can gather, he was pleased with the toughness of his college and delighted in the strong contrast he provided. "We don't think much of Pater here" an official of the college remarked to me a year or two ago.

Games-playing as the college is, a tradition of manners survives. Ten or fifteen years ago, when Oxford was sharply divided into aesthetes and hearties, an aesthete was not safe in Brasenose. An aesthete friend of the writer gauged the true tradition of sportsmanship which still lingers in the college. Though sound in his limbs, he would always walk through the quadrangles limping on a stick because, he said, "the hearties would be too sporting to attack a lame aesthete".

CAMPION HALL is a Jesuit foundation below Pembroke College. It is named after Edmund Campion and the present buildings in stone with a rather unfortunate red roof were designed by Sir Edwin Lutyens—the only example of that architect's work in Oxford. The chapel is interesting as showing what may be done with a small space; so is the general plan of the buildings.

CANAL. The Oxford Canal was an early nineteenth century project and adds beauty to the bricky skirt of the stationside of Oxford. Its wharf, whither barges once came from Banbury, Coventry and the Grand Union Canal, is the proposed site of "Nuffield College". A particularly fine Greek Revival house surveyed the wharf just below Bulwark's Lane.

CARFAX is that junction of the four main streets in the town (Corn Market, Queen Street, St. Ald's and the High) at which every visitor finds himself sooner or later, waiting for the traffic lights. The architecture of the four corners equally divided between Edwardian-Jacobo-Rococo and refined neo-Tudor. The heavily restored, mediaeval church tower is all that remains of St. Martin's Church. The nave looks, from engravings, to have been a good specimen of early perpendicular revival (1822). It was demolished in 1896.

CASTLE. Oxford Castle is almost impossible to visit without a deal of letter-writing beforehand, because it stands in the ground of the prison. The tower, a late Norman construction which looks as old as the oldest antiquarian would wish, frowns above a branch of the river which here winds up to its base from Folly Bridge, after an interesting tour of the backs of small factories. The character of this part of Oxford, grey stone castle tower above small squalid red houses, has been destroyed by slum clearance and the removal of the mill (pre-Conquest in origin) a year or two ago, which stood beneath the Castle Tower. In its place a little suburban garden has been planted by that dainty miss, municipal enterprise.

Within the castle precincts are a Saxon mound and a Norman crypt.

Up the lane to St. Giles from the castle was once a fine late eighteenth century house now disfigured by cement covering. Beyond that is an unexplained Baroque doorway in a garden wall.

CATHEDRAL is certainly disappointing. "'Tis truly no elegant structure"* and it stands in a corner behind Tom Quad in Christ Church. Had Wolsey completed his great schemes for Christ Church, the Cathedral might have been one of the most notable Perpendicular buildings in England, a rival to King's Chapel, Cambridge. As it is, it is a condensed collection of various styles of Gothic architecture, of more delight to the antiquarian than to the appreciator of architecture.

Indeed it is smaller than most cathedrals and a good many abbeys. The best view of its exterior is from the Fellows garden of Christ Church or the back gardens of some of the Canons' houses on the Cathedral side of Tom Quad. The dumpy spire is pure E.E., and was the admiration of Ruskin.

The east end is an arrangement of windows in the Norman manner made by Sir Gilbert Scott in 1871. This takes the place of an enamelled window attributed to Sir James Thornhill. Oxford Cathedral had perhaps the best collection of seventeenth

* Browne Wills, *Survey of Cathedrals* 1730.

OXFORD CATHEDRAL IN THE EARLY NINETEENTH CENTURY

and eighteenth century stained and painted glass in any English ecclesiastical building. Most of it was removed in the last century except for that mentioned under (3) and (5). In the last century, too, the nave was filled with the present seating arrangements.

Its best features are:

(1) The Perpendicular roof of the choir with elaborate stone vaulting.

(2) The Becket window (fourteenth century) in south transept.

(3) The window, west end north aisle of nave by the Younger Van Linge (seventeenth century). It represents Jonah and the Gourd with Nineveh in the background. Notice the greens and blues. This is one of the handsomest stained glass windows in Oxford.

(4) The St. Frideswide window by Burne-Jones (1858) in the Latin Chapel. This is his best work, feeble in colour compared with Van Linge, but infinitely better than the other ghastly windows here and elsewhere in Oxford by Burne-Jones and Morris.

(5) Bishop King's Tomb and window (seventeenth century) in south aisle.

(6) St. Frideswide's shrine-base, recently restored.

(7) Robert Burton's Monument.

(8) The organ case (1680).

The exposed masonry near the St. Frideswide's shrine is post-Conquest, not Saxon as was long supposed.

Outside there are some good late Perpendicular cloisters and a restored, but still somewhat Early English chapter house, approached by a rich Norman door.

Christ Church.

BUILDINGS. Christ Church was founded by Cardinal Wolsey, hence the Cardinal's hat on some of the buildings and on the writing paper. But Wolsey was disgraced before he could complete his scheme of making the college at once a monument to his munificence and to Tudor architecture.

Two large quadrangles, Peckwater and Tom Quad, the latter the largest in

PECKWATER QUAD, CH: CH: *c.* 1705

Oxford, almost touch one another. The best approach to the college is by way of Canterbury Gate in Merton Street; thence the glories of Christ Church unfold, and of these glories, the classic are the more magnificent, for the Tudor were never finished.

The massive Doric gateway which faces you in Merton Street was built by James Wyatt in 1778. He too designed the small quadrangle in which you find yourself, called Canterbury Quad. Your eye will be arrested by the enormous black library immediately opposite Canterbury Gate and which dominates this part of the college. This building, with three-quarter Corinthian columns of huge dimensions all along it, was designed by the able amateur architect, Dr. George Clarke, more of whose work may be seen at All Souls and Worcester Colleges. The library was building 1716–1761. The architect's original intention was to leave the lower storey open, as was intended at the Queen's College, Oxford, and Trinity, Cambridge, and to have an open piazza of seven arches commanding a view of the cathedral and approached by three steps along the ascent of the building.*

Apart from the collection of drawings and MSS which the library contains, a collection which, with that of the Ashmolean,

* "Fortunately the ground floor was subsequently filled in, as the original design would have been painfully out of keeping with the surroundings." Observation in Ward Lock's *Oxford*, Current Edition, 1937.

makes a superb survey of Italian and German art; apart from this, the library should certainly be seen. The statues and busts by eminent eighteenth century sculptors, is remarkable. I would say that except for Queen's College Library, the Christ Church Library on the first floor is the most beautiful room in Oxford, especially on a sunny day with the light streaming on to the plaster work from an end window. In the words of *The Oxford University and City Guide* (N.D. c. 1820) "Its fitting up is in a fine taste; and the festoons of stucco are charged with symbols, exquisitely worked, of the particular branch of learning over which they are placed. The ceiling is richly ornamented; and the wainscotting and pillars are of the finest Norway oak".

The buildings which bound the other three sides of this quadrangle, called Peckwater, were designed by Dean Aldrich (see All Saints Church), another amateur architect, in about 1705. With the library, so much out of scale with Dean Aldrich's work as not to compete with it, this forms a noble classic composition. You may get a fine view by standing about thirty paces out from the centre of the library into Peckwater Quad and turning towards Canterbury Gate. Merton Tower is in the background and the divergent classic compositions of the eighteenth century centre on Canterbury Gate, parts of which may be seen, moulding together the library and Dean Aldrich's buildings.

In compliance with the prevailing fashion grass has been laid down in Peckwater Quad in place of the gravel which formed so excellent a base in the past and gave an Italian air to the quad.

A turn to the left at the far end of the library (notice the sundial on the wall of the Dean's house) leads to an archway. Here

CHRIST CHURCH, ST. ALDATE'S FRONT AND TOM TOWER

Tom Quad spreads out before you. Its effect to me has always been more of size than of beauty. The buildings around it, except Tom Tower and Christ Church Hall are undistinguished and I wish that the cloister, the bases for buttresses and pilasters of which you may see all along, had been completed.

The diminutive fountain in the middle is known as Mercury and toughs sometimes dip men less tough in the pond which surrounds it.

If you walk straight down towards the hall you will come, on your left, to the obscure entrance to Oxford's Cathedral (which see under separate heading). This Diocesan Cathedral, is also the college chapel. The most interesting architectural feature of Christ Church, and, next to the library, the most beautiful, is the staircase to the hall. Notice the purple grey of the stone, the riddling decoration, the broad, shallow steps, the strange and satisfactory proportions. Of all Gothic things in Oxford, this is the most curious. Not only is it the most curious, but it is also among the latest consciously "Gothic" works to be found in England, as it was constructed in 1640. The single clustered column which seems to support the roof is certainly constructional but it does not support as much of the fan vaulting as the designer of that vaulting would have us believe. The vaulting is mostly false, the ribs being fixed on as a decorative

Corbel at the entrance to St. John's College (sixteenth century).

St. John's College, late seventeenth century colonnade.

feature disguised as a constructive one. But the lace-like intricacy is completely successful.

Up the stairs is Christ Church Hall, the finest Gothic dining hall in Oxford. Its oak roof (1529 and 1720) must have been seen to more advantage before the windows beneath were filled with unfortunate Victorian stained glass. A few armorial bearings here and there would have been excellent. But now there is too little light.

The portraits on the walls are good, especially those by Kneller, Gainsborough, Reynolds, Lawrence, Orchardson and Shee, and Millais' portrait of Gladstone, but G. F. Watts' Dean Liddell (of Liddell and Scott fame) is not up to his excellent earlier portraits. Some other good portraits are in a room used by the Canons near the Chapter House.

The dons sit on the dais and disappear with their table napkins to port and coffee through a door in the wall which leads down to a senior common room. The undergraduates sit at the tables below the dais.

Once more pass down the shallow stairs beneath that fan-vaulting, go through the three-quarter cloister, noticing windows on the side which may be the work of Wren, come out under a tower and you will find yourself before a large Gothic Revival pile called Meadow Buildings which gave place to some decent seventeenth century buildings of Dr. Fell's reign. The present buildings were built from the designs of Sir Thomas Deane of the firm of Deane & Woodward (see also the University Museum) in 1862. They represent, according to Mr. E. A. Greening Lamborn,* the result in stone of the mistaken doctrine

*Handbook of the University of Oxford, 1934, pp. 66-7.

that Venetian Gothic was the only genuine article, which was being preached with fatal eloquence by Ruskin. The Meadow Buildings are the memorial of Dean Liddell's reign as Dean of Christ Church. They certainly should be seen, as curiosities, as a bold Gothic block, singularly gloomy to live in, yet so vividly Ruskin's dream as to be preferable to the faint hearted attempts at Neo - Gothic - moderno - classicism practised by well-known architects in present day Oxford. Meadow Buildings are an honest expression of the gas-enlightened 'sixties. As such, they are worthy of preservation. There is nothing quite like them, except the University Museum, now that the Post Office has been Tudorized.

The Broad Walk is good from Meadow Buildings. Christ Church Hall looks fine from the ill-planned little garden that has just been planted by the College, connecting the Broad Walk with St. Aldates.

If you leave by the skimpy gates of this garden, cross the road towards Bishop King's Palace (q.v.) and look up at the fine front of Christ Church, up the hill on the opposite side. Tom Tower, which holds this Tudor composition together, is by Wren. The Tudor part is by Wolsey. Wolsey never finished the gateway and it was for Wren to put the top on it. Tom Tower (1681) is far the most successful of Wren's Gothic works. No Gothic architect, of course, ever dreamed of such detail or such shape. But the tower is none the less successful for that.

Within the Tower is Great Tom, a mediaeval bell from Osney Abbey, recast in 1680. At 9 by Oxford time (which is 9.5 by Greenwich time) Tom strikes 101 strokes and all college gates throughout Oxford are shut. Thereafter, undergraduates may only get in by kicking at the

CHRIST CHURCH HALL. TEMP: HENRY VIII

doors of their colleges and waiting for the porter to open to them. Christ Church men are allowed in by this kicking method until 12.20. I have no idea why.

Take one more look at this fine front of Christ Church as you walk up the hill to Carfax. Notice how squarely the whole building strides the hill.

PEOPLE. The make-up of Christ Church is curious, for the Cathedral is a diocesan building with a bishop, who lives outside Oxford in the semi-rurality of Cuddesdon, and a Dean who is also head of the College. There are Canons attached to the Cathedral, some of whom live in the houses in Tom Quad with their wives and families. There are also dons living in the College. The dons and the Canons have not always hit it off, but on the whole the arrangement works well.

GENTLEMEN.

Sir Philip Sidney (1554–1586).

Richard Hakluyt (1552(?)–1616).

Richard Allestree (1619–1681), author of *The Whole Duty of Man*.

John Locke (1632–1704) took philosophically the deprivations of his studentship because he was a Whig, by order of the King. See the Kneller portrait in the hall.

William Penn (1644–1718). Quaker and colonist.

Dean Aldrich (1647–1710), Beautifier of Oxford by means of Palladian Architecture (Peckwater Quad and All Saints Church his chief works): musician: composed "the Bonnie Christ Church Bells": smoked tobacco and the round is said to give space for each singer to pull at his pipe and so keep it alight during singing. The bells themselves are in the late Victorian tower over the hall staircase.

John Wesley (1703–1791). Turn to Lincoln College to which he migrated to a Fellowship.

Charles Wesley (1707–1788).

Lord Mansfield (1705–1793), Lord Chief Justice.

George Canning (1770–1827), statesman and humorous poet.

> "But of all plagues, good heaven, thy wrath can send,
>   Save, save, oh! save me from the candid friend."

Lord Canning (1812–1862), Governor-General of India.

Sir Robert Peel (1788–1850), first to win a double first under the Examination Statute brought about by Dean Cyril Jackson.

George Colman the elder (1732–1794).

George Colman the younger (1762–1836).

Rev. C. L. Dodgson ("Lewis Carroll"), (1832–98) mathematical don and author of *Alice in Wonderland*.

Rev. Edward Bouverie Pusey (1800–1882).

F. Augustus John Smith (1804–1872), revived the Scilly Islands.

John Ruskin (1819–1900), hence Meadow Buildings.

W. E. Gladstone (1809–1898), double first, of course.

Martin F. Tupper (1810–1889), *Proverbial Philosophy*.

WELL-KNOWN DEANS OF CHRIST CHURCH.

Rev. Thomas Sampson (1517?–1589), Calvinist.

Rev. Samuel Fell (1584–1649).

Rev. John Fell (1625–1686), disciplinarian and examination pioneer: subject of Tom Brown's well-known adaptation of Martial's *Non amo te, Sabidi*.

Rev. Henry Aldrich (see above under People).

Rev. Francis Atterbury (1663–1732), fiery Protestant. Famous for scholarly feud with Bentley of Cambridge.

Rev. Cyril Jackson (1746–1819), chiefly responsible for "Public Examination Statute" which started the pre-occupation of dons with the subject of "first-class brains". Said to Gaisford, a future dean, "You will never be a gentleman, but you may succeed with certainty as a scholar".*

Thomas Gaisford (1779–1855), fulfilled Cyril Jackson's prophecy.

Henry George Liddell (1811–1898), Greek-English Lexicon. Subject of one of Thomas Hardy's only humorous poems.

Christ Church is the grandest of the colleges. It contains the most "Bullingdon Men". It has been described as a large hotel. It is less troubled by "college spirit" than other colleges. It has an ancient connection with Westminster, and when Eton eclipsed that school it received, and still receives with open arms, people from Eton.

* Francis Gribble: *The Romance of Oxford Colleges*.

UNIVERSITY PRESS, WALTON STREET.   DANIEL ROBERTSON, ARCH: 1830

The colloquial name of Christ Church is the House. It is written Ch: Ch:

CLARENDON BUILDING is that enormous four-columned building beneath which the proctors interview undergraduates and where that odd thing, the Oxford University Chest, has its little office. The building (1711–1724) is attributed to Vanbrugh, on what authority I do not know, for it is more like the work of Hawksmoor, who was paid for it. A house, which really may be by Vanbrugh, exists opposite the Union in St. Michael's Street.

The Clarendon Building originally housed the Clarendon Press, which printed, as it still prints, University publications.

It is certainly the most handsome building in Broad Street and one can only hope that the refined extension of the Bodleian opposite has not ruined its present excellent proportion to the street. Notice the wrought iron gates, contemporary with the building.

CLARENDON PRESS is a handsome series of buildings in Walton Street. Three large projecting blocks in the Corinthian order are joined by a classic screen. The date of these buildings is 1830 and the architect was Daniel Robertson, who reconstructed the south front of All Souls, and the St. Mary Hall part of Oriel.

There is not space here to go into the history of the Clarendon or Oxford University Press. Its present revenue is derived from Bibles and children's books (the latter published under the name of Humphrey Milford) and the profits on these help to pay for learned publications.

ST. CLEMENT'S CHURCH. Is a charming pseudo - Norman composition which rises from the Cherwell meadows opposite Addison's Walk. It was built 1827–1828 by Daniel Robertson and has always been old-fashioned Evangelical.

REV. HENRY B. BULTEEL,
Preaching at St. Ebbe's, A.D 1833

Mr Bulteel, Fellow and Tutor of Exeter College, was sometime Curate of St Ebbe's, Oxford. He seceded from the Established Church and founded this Chapel in 1832, at a cost of £4,000

THE IRVINGITE CLERGYMAN FROM EXETER COLLEGE. A SILHOUETTE NOW IN THE POSSESSION OF THE TRUSTEES OF THE COMMERCIAL ROAD BAPTIST CHURCH

As you go down Headington Hill and arrive in the rather squalid purlieus of St. Clements, a handsome row of almshouses built of limestone appear on your left. These are called Stone's Almshouses and were built in 1700 for eight poor widows. They are among the only worthy buildings left in St. Clement's.

Beyond Mágdalen and by the Bridge,
on a place called there the Plain
In Summer, in a burst of summer-
time,
Following falls and falls of rain,
When the air was sweet-and-sour
of the flown fine flower of
Those goldnails and their gaylinks that
hang along a lime;*

To-day three main, petrol blue roads converge at this, the western extremity of St. Clement's.

COLLEGE BARGES are found along the Thames by Christ Church meadow. In the interests of specialization, extended even to rowing, it is being thought expedient to do away with them and build nice up-to-date pavilions instead.

The Barges are a relic of Georgian times. They certainly existed in 1825, though not the present boats. On no aesthetic grounds can their abolition be justified, not even on the rather futile plea of opening up yet another "view". The Barges are really floating changing rooms, with flat roofs for spectators of rowing events.

Rowing men are said to object to "the peculiarly unpleasant smells of the changing room, an ancient and complicated odour composed of ingredients I forbear to analyse too closely"—letter from a rowing don in *Oxford*, Spring, 1936.

COMMERCIAL ROAD BAPTIST CHURCH. An octagonal building which is no longer a place of worship, in the early industrial surroundings below St. Ebbe's. Built in 1831 for the Rev. H. B. Bulteel (1800–1866), a Fellow of Exeter, who had left the C. of E. for Irvingism.

* G. M. Hopkins.

CONGREGATION HOUSE (see St. Mary-the-Virgin).

CONVOCATION HOUSE. Is best approached from the west end of the Divinity Schools. Built 1634–1640 in Archbishop Laud's time. On these uncomfortable benches sat the Commons in 1665 during the Civil Wars. On them now sit senior members of the University to discuss University business. The treble bell in St. Mary's Church is rung and the members, in gowns, but not hoods, file into the benches. Meetings are held on every Tuesday, except the first, of full term. There is a sundial in seventeenth century glass in the window opposite the Divinity Schools entrance.

Corpus Christi College.

BUILDINGS. So beautiful is the description by Bishop Foxe of this small, but not dim college, that I must quote it. Bishop

Foxe (1448?–1528), not the martyrologist, but the predecessor of Wolsey in Henry VIII's confidence, founded "Corpus", as it is called, in 1516. This is quoted by Dr. Wells in Methuen's *Little Guide to Oxford and Its Colleges* as Foxe's description of his college. " 'We have no continuing city here, but seek one that shall be in heaven, to which we hope to arrive more easily and quickly if we raise a ladder, calling its right side virtue and its left knowledge.' He

therefore founds a college wherein 'as in a hive', 'the scholars, like clever bees night and day may make wax and sweet honey to the honour of God and the advantage of themselves and all Christian men' ! "

Greek was once compulsory in Corpus. The reputation for scholarship still remains. The college is rich out of proportion to its size.

The Quadrangle one enters from Merton Street is undistinguished, typical early sixteenth century work, over-restored on the Merton Street front. What proportions there were, were destroyed in the eighteenth century, when the present buildings were raised a storey. Before then, the sundial (1581) surmounted by a pelican, must have looked well and given some unity to the quadrangle. What texture of wall surface it had was destroyed in the beginning of the nineteenth century when the walls were faced with Barrington stone, replacing the plaster and rough-cast.

The hall, on your left from the Merton Street entrance, was unfortunately re-Gothicized in the middle of the last century. Its open roof (1525), early eighteenth century panelling and portraits, especially that of Foxe, are worth seeing and so far as one is able to see them in the wretched light.

The chapel, redolent of cedar wood, is too dark. If the Victorian stained glass were removed, it would be revealed for the charming building it is. The black and white marble pavement would set off once more the dark woodwork, and the decent altar piece (ascribed to Rubens) would come into its own, so would the massive screen. This chapel is really a simplified version of the exquisite and unspoiled one at Lincoln College.

The library runs all along the south side of the quadrangle. It is almost equal with

Merton and Jesus libraries in its air of early-Renaissance scholarship undisturbed by any noise save the buzz of flies, and any odours save those of leather and woodwork. It contains many rare seventeenth century

temporary with the cloister and should be seen from the Meadow side. It is ascribed to Dean Aldrich. The rooms in it on its first floor are well proportioned and with the best views in Oxford. Though

CORPUS CHRISTI, TURNER'S NEW BUILDING (*c.* 1710)
HERE RUSKIN HAD ROOMS

books and is, to the bibliophile, one of the most important libraries of Oxford. See the illuminated MSS history of the Bible, given in its superb binding by General Oglethorpe.

Beyond the chapel is a cloister (1706) adorned with marble monuments. It extends along the chapel wall and is a classic fortaste of the excellent Fellows Building or Turner's Building opposite. This is con-

Ruskin had rooms here, he encouraged Meadow Buildings, Christ Church. Should the projected road be driven through Christ Church Meadows, this, the best part of Oxford, will be permanently spoiled. It was on Ch: Ch: Meadows that Dr. Johnson skated on the ice.

The college plate survived melting down during the civil wars and may still be seen.

The salt cellar of blue and green enamel and silver gilt (c. 1517) is the most exquisite piece of metal work in Oxford. Bishop Foxe's crozier, same date and style, is nearly, but not quite, up to the standard of the crozier at New College.

PEOPLE.

Nicholas Udall (1505–1556), Headmaster of Eton, a flogger, author of *Ralph Roister Doister*, an early comedy read by English students.

Rev. John Jewel (1522–1571), Fellow. See Merton.

Richard Hooker (1554?–1600), "Judicious Theologian". Made an injudicious marriage and had to give up his fellowship.

Duke of Monmouth (1649–1685).

General Oglethorpe (1696–1785), founded the state of Georgia.

Edward Young (went to All Souls, q.v.).

John Keble (1792–1866), High Churchman, author of *Christian Year*. Is said to have damaged the Sundial at Corpus by throwing a bottle at it.

Thomas Arnold (1795–1842), Headmaster of Rugby, "we might be, indeed we were, somewhat boyish in manner, and in the liberties we took with each other . . . our habits were inexpensive and temperate. . . ." Letter from Sir John Taylor Coleridge (1790–1876), also of Corpus, in Dean Stanley's *Life of Dr. Arnold*.

Henry Nettleship (1839–1893), Professor of Latin.

Sir Henry Newbolt (1862–1938), Poet. See *My World as in My Time*.

COUNTY HALL stands opposite the proposed site of "Nuffield College" and has a fanciful façade in the Norman style of 1840 by J. Plowman. Behind the façade are Assize Courts. Before it, some excellent iron railings. The whole has the effect of an early lithograph and a quality so strong that one feels certain our friend Progress will soon set to work refining it or pulling it down. Other examples of the Norman Revival in Oxford are St. Clement's Church (1827, but repaired and beautified within), Kennington Church (1828) and it would hardly be stretching a point to say Iffley Church (c. 1150 and c. 1860).

COWLEY was once a village, is now a suburb created mostly by the Morris works (see p. 155) and indistinguishable from any other suburb of a post-war industrial town.

The one building worth seeing in Cowley is Mr. J. N. Comper's Chapel (1906) for the Hospital of St. John behind the church of SS. Mary and John. It was undoubtedly the inspiration for Temple Moore's Chapel to Pusey House and with that ranks as the best twentieth century Gothic in Oxford.

Down the Iffley Road is G. F. Bodley's Church of St. John the Evangelist (1896) erected for the Cowley Fathers. The plain tower facing the road is original and impressive, the church inside is less successful. The services are well sung.

ST. CROSS CHURCH, tolling to the many distinguished brains now gone to dust in Holywell cemetery, stands by "Balliol Manor", a decent new annexe to Balliol College (architect, George Kennedy) among the recreation grounds above Holywell. The church tower has a handsome sundial on it. The church is an interesting specimen, within, of re-decoration in the

St. John's College Gardens (*above*).
Eighteenth century wrought iron gates to New College Gardens (*below*).

Keble College (1870), by William Butterfield, a great Gothic revival architect, at his best. A monochrome photograph, such as this, shows up the originality of his detail and his excellent sense of proportion: it lessens the violence of his colour scheme and juxtaposition of textures.

1890 manner. There is an eleventh century chancel arch and little else of antiquity. The churchyard has some good plain early nineteenth century stones. In 1624 Thomas Holt of York was buried in this churchyard. He is said to have built the "Tower of the Five Orders" in the Old Schools building, which now houses part of the Bodleian.

DIVINITY SCHOOL. The masons who built Oxford's Divinity School (c. 1430–1483) were called Winchcombe and Orchard. For the summit of the mediaeval course of learning, it was appropriate that the most magnificent building should be built. Mr. Rice Oxley quotes Sir Roger Wilbraham, a judge, as saying in 1603 "The chiefest Wonder in Oxford is a faire Divinitie School with church windoes:

and over it the fairest librarie". The Divinity School is still the chiefest wonder, and not the most confirmed admirer of the Renaissance can fail to acknowledge this as the happiest construction of stone and glass in the University.

Enter the great quadrangle that holds the Bodleian and turn to the west, with your back to the Tower of the Orders (1612–1619). That panelled space divided into thin, decorative compartments ranged to emphasize the horizontal construction of this part of the building, marks the west front of the school and Duke Humphrey's rich library above it.

Without a doubt it is the most effective side of this rather gloomy quadrangle. As Mr. Madan points out in *Oxford Outside the Guide Books* here, "written for ever in stone is the whole course of mediaeval

QUEEN'S LANE, WITH ST. EDMUND HALL ON RIGHT AND ST. PETER'S-IN-THE-EAST BEYOND IT

education". Behind you is its initial faculty of the arts. Before you, on your left, is the door to the old School of Medicine, on your right the School of Jurisprudence, and in the middle, the School of Theology. All ways lead eventually to God.

As a foretaste of heaven, this central entrance gives on to the Proscholium. This is now sometimes called the pig market. In the days of religious dissension, during Edward VI's reign, the Divinity School was disused and was not properly repaired until the seventeenth century. Brambles and nettles grew against the walls: the stained glass was smashed: the citizens of Oxford used it, and its neighbourhood, for a market for pigs and as an airing ground for laundry.

The Proscholium now has a Protestant austerity, softened by the mellow quality of the stone, especially when the afternoon sunlight streams at an angle through the south window and is reflected on the vaulting; this austerity is relieved by the stone panelled walls and by the elaborate entrance door to the school itself.

The interior causes the same gasp of wonder as comes on first entering King's College Chapel, Cambridge. Such delicate masonry, so much branching vaulting, flowing with bosses and dangling into pendants, the columns rising up the walls with such multiplex precision! Nowhere does the quality of slightly weathered stonework show to better advantage in Oxford. The skilfully contrived door in Renaissance Gothic which daringly breaks through a window on the Sheldonian side was executed by Bird who worked for Wren.

ST. EBBE's is a district behind the south side of Queen Street and with still some of the Oxford town architecture of the past in its lanes. The church, very Low, has a beak-head Norman door, but nothing else of architectural interest.

St. Edmund Hall.

BUILDINGS. A collection of pleasant, undistinguished and partly ancient buildings in Queen's Lane just below St. Peter's in the east church. In this lane there used

to be a notice with a typically Oxford plural "No chars-a-banc allowed here". The only block with pretentions to architecture in the little quadrangle is the chapel and library (1680–1682) facing the entrance. Attenuated pilasters run up the centre of the block and support a diminutive pediment. The chapel, a dark building, with good woodwork, is not improved by the Burne-Jones stained window—said to be his first. The library over the ante-chapel has been found to contain many valuable theological books. It is a charming galleried room.

PEOPLE. St. Edmund's is the last of the old halls of which there were once (1440) eighty-four in Oxford. The halls came before the colleges, in the development of the University. They were often absorbed into colleges. Among the last to go in the nineteenth century were St. Mary Hall (Skimmery), New Inn Hall (The Tavern), St. Alban Hall (Stubbin's), Magdalen Hall ("seedy Magdalen"). They were rather looked down upon. St. Edmund Hall (Teddy Hall) has had a hard fight to save itself from absorption into The Queen's College across the lane.

> John Kettlewell (1653–1695), High Church Divine.
>
> John Oldham (1653–1683), Poet.
> "Lord of myself, accountable to none But to my Conscience, and my God alone."
>
> Thomas Hearne (1678–1735), Antiquarian and diarist of Oxford scandal to whom all Oxford guide book writers are indebted.
>
> Daniel Wilson (1816–1892), Evangelical Bishop of Calcutta.
>
> Sir John Stainer (1840–1901), Composer of sacred music.

ELLISTON & CAVELL'S restaurant is a place of meeting for North Oxford ladies and undergraduates (not necessarily at the same tables).

EXAMINATION SCHOOLS. An enormous Jacobethan pile in the High Street and with a front in Merton Street which would look well in mahogany and looking glass. It is the apex of the Anglo-Jackson style and was designed by Sir Thomas Jackson and opened in 1882. The carved panel over the portico of an undergraduate being hit over the head by a book is worth noting.

The interior is exceedingly well planned and the light and depressing rooms have been the scene of much unhappiness. The small tables have drawings on them in ink by undergraduates who were clearly to be ploughed, whiling away their time when there were questions they could not answer.

Exeter College.

BUILDINGS. The Turl front was Gothicized by H. J. Underwood in 1835. The vaulting of the porch is good seventeenth century work, but I

do not advise visitors to look further who are not interested in the Gothic Revival as conceived by Sir Gilbert Scott. True the hall was built in 1618 and some parts of the entrance quadrangle are in the usual late mediaeval style. But the college is dominated by Sir Gilbert Scott, an architect who had more work to do than he had talent to carry out. The chapel (1856–1859) is regarded as his *chef d'oeuvre* and it is certainly elaborate. The interior, dark with wondrous 1860 glass, prickly with stalls by G. F. Bodley at his worst, contains a tapestry by Burne Jones and William Morris. But it is not seen to advantage in these dark, vaulted, French Decorated surroundings. The chapel as a whole is said to recall Sainte Chapelle and Lichfield Cathedral. It displays no originality of design, the vaulting at the east end being exceedingly poor— Pearson could have done better—and the proportions unsatisfactory because the length of the building seems to be truncated and overcrowded. Its best feature is the flèche seen from Ship Street.

Beyond the chapel is a Gothic quadrangle by Sir Gilbert with rooms and staircases reminiscent of a Peabody Building. It is this part of Exeter College which elbows out the Old Ashmolean in Broad Street. The library in Methodist Decorated replaced a charming eighteenth century building in 1856. The best thing about the college is the chestnut tree which overhangs the wall of the Fellows Garden.

There is a suggestion that the Broad Street front of Exeter College is to be demolished. Let us hope that its successor will not be in the inevitable twentieth century sham-Renaissance or refined-Tudor.

P E O P L E. The college has west country connections. It is also connected in my mind with the High Church party.

The first Lord Shaftesbury (1621–1683). "When the senior fellows designed to alter the beer of the college, which was stronger than other colleges, I hindered the design." He also put down the "tucking" of freshmen "it having been a foolish custom of great antiquity that one of the seniors in the evening called the freshmen . . . to the fire and made them hold out their chin and they, with the nail of their right thumb, left long for that purpose, grate off all the skin from the lip to the chin, and then caused them to drink a beer glass of water and salt".

In the eighteenth century the college was said to be given over to drink and Whiggery. Merton was the other Whig College.

James Anthony Froude (1818–1894), the historian, was a Fellow of Exeter, 1842–1849. His High Church brother, Richard Hurrell Froude, fellow of Oriel, roped him into the Newman coterie and was probably responsible for his being asked by J. H. Newman to contribute a "Life of St. Neot" to the *Lives of the Saints*. J. A. Froude is said to have ended his essay with the words "This is all, and probably more than all,

that is known of the life of the blessed St. Neot". Newman was deeply offended, so were the High Church party. Froude later resigned his fellowship out of pique because of the public burning of his book *The Nemesis of Faith*.

Francis Turner Palgrave (1824–1897), Fellow 1847. Edited *Golden Treasury*. Professor of Poetry.

William Morris (1834–1896) and Sir Edward Burne Jones (1833–1898) were undergraduates together at Exeter. Here they formed the friendship, bringing in Swinburne from over the way at Balliol, which started the Pre-Raphaelite Brotherhood. Morris was known as "Topsy" and was described by his tutor as "a rather rough and unpolished youth who exhibited no special literary tastes or capacity but had no difficulty in mastering the usual subjects of examinations".

S T. G I L E S' is the broad thoroughfare out of which branch the Banbury and Woodstock Roads, either side of St. Giles' Church. The whole area is covered with a fair early in September (see Chap: I). The church, at the northern end, which has a countrified look, is of interest to antiquarians. It is a stronghold of "Broad Church" teaching.

Hertford College.

B U I L D I N G S. The entrance quadrangle contains an Elizabethan dining hall changed to a library, and a Jacobean block of no distinction opposite the entrance. Some decent early nineteenth century blocks flank the main entrance, but they are not improved by an extraordinary staircase between them, in imitation of Blois, designed by Sir Thomas Jackson who did the chapel (1908), and the "Bridge of Sighs" over New College Lane (1913).

PEOPLE. Hertford College was resuscitated in 1874, having been Magdalen Hall before that. In the eighteenth century

it had been called Hertford College, thanks to the efforts of Dr. Newton (1676–1753), an excitable and prolific writer on educational matters—a pioneer of educational reform, who wanted to change Hart Hall, of which he was principal, into Hertford College. He had a great row with Balliol. "I am not willing that either *Baliol*, or any *other college* whatsoever, should be thought a *cheaper* place to live in than *Hart Hall*, because I do not think it possible." Dr. Newton got his Hertford College by charter in 1740. It did not last long. The story of its end is sad " . . . by 1805 there were only two Fellows and no pupils left; in 1814 one surviving Fellow who was considered 'half-cracked', 'nominated, constituted and admitted himself Principal'; in 1820 the buildings on Cat Street (where the main entrance is now) fell down with a great crash and a dense cloud of dust.* Magdalen Hall removed here in 1820 when its buildings beside Magdalen College were burned down.

John Donne (1573–1631) was at Hart Hall which he entered very young so

* *Oxford Renowned*, L. Rice Oxley.

as to avoid taking the Oath of Supremacy.

John Selden (1584–1654), Jurist at Hart Hall.

Dr. Robert Plot (1640–1696), Antiquary and topographer.

Charles James Fox (1749–1806) was at the 1st Hertford College. Is said to have jumped from his window into Cat Street to take part in a town and gown row.

John Meade Falkner (1858–1932), Novelist, antiquarian and armaments manufacturer, wrote *The Lost Stradivarius*, a ghost story about Oxford and Italy.

HOLY TRINITY CHURCH was built in the E.E. style of 1845. It is near the gasworks, Low, and redolent of the works, hassocks and old copies of the Hymnal Companion. A complete survival of Victorian architecture and furnishing which should be preserved.

INDIAN INSTITUTE, founded in 1883 for "The work of fostering and facilitating Indian studies in this University; the work of making Englishmen, and even Indians themselves, appreciate better than they have done before the languages, literature and industries of India". To this end the architect, Mr. Basil Champneys, built the everlasting yellow building on the corner of Holywell and Broad Street, "in the style of the English Renaissance, with some Oriental details" (1894–1896). Some of these details have lately been shaved off.

Jesus College.

BUILDINGS. The front opposite Exeter is a good specimen of Gothic Revival work (1856) by J. C. Buckler.

The two quadrangles which form most of the college are grassed squares surrounded by what look like Cotswold manors on all sides. The clearness of the planning of Jesus College and the relation of the heights of the buildings to the size of the quadrangles make what would be undistinguished buildings judged on their

detail, into something distinguished. The buildings were judiciously altered in 1815. The chapel (early seventeenth century) has a fine classic screen and a good brass lectern of eighteenth century date which somehow survived a fearful "restoration" by G. E. Street in 1864.

The hall, with the usual panelling and elaborate screen (seventeenth century), contains two portraits which should certainly be seen. One is of Queen Elizabeth, a founder of this college, a singularly delicate work (notice the wild strawberry she is wearing)* and the other is a portrait by Sir Thomas Lawrence of the great architect John Nash who did some work for the college. (John Nash was not at the college, but Beau Nash was.) The library looks as though it had been untouched and not a book removed since 1677 when most of it was built. The woodwork, the brown leather of the books, the clear windows and the slim height of the room make it one of the best little-known sights of Oxford.

Some dull buildings in a Perpendicular style (1906) face Ship Street.

* There is another portrait of Queen Elizabeth in the Senior Common Room.

PEOPLE. Jesus College is, and always has been, associated with Wales. Nearly everyone in it is supposed to be called Jones. There is an exclusiveness about Jesus College which it is hard to explain unless it be that the Welsh stick together like Plymouth Brethren.

An interesting fact about Jesus College is that it holds the key to the replanning of London because it owns considerable land along the south bank of the Thames opposite Charing Cross.

Lancelot Andrewes (1555–1626), Bishop of Winchester, buried in Southwark Cathedral, was an early Fellow.

James Howell (1593–1666).

Henry Vaughan (1622–1695), left without taking his degree: so did Beau Nash (1674–1762), but for making arrangements, while an undergraduate of under seventeen, to marry a girl.

Rev. John Richard Green (1837–1883), Historian.

THE HALL AND SECOND QUAD, JESUS COLLEGE

Sir Lewis Morris (1833–1907), Minor poet and educationalist. Feeling that his work was unappreciated he is said to have remarked to Wilde, "Oscar, what would you advise me to do in the face of this conspiracy of silence?" "I would advise you to join the conspiracy."*

* Quoted by Francis Gribble in *The Romance of Oxford Colleges*.

St. John's College.

BUILDINGS. St. John's College in St. Giles has a low stone wall in front of it, shaped like a fender and protecting some gigantic elms from the stream of

traffic into Oxford from the north. There is a legend that the bulldogs cannot arrest an undergraduate and bring him before the proctors once he has escaped to this fender. Similar fenders once existed before Balliol and Trinity. The front and south side of the first quadrangle are partly fifteenth century. On the left is the hall, a sixteenth century building improved in Georgian times. The kitchens near the hall are early seventeenth century. The chapel is a continuation of the hall eastwards. It was consecrated in 1530, but a Gothic "restoration" by Edward Blore 300 years later has altered its character. The Gothic, though not inspired, is pleasant enough to look at, so far as one is able to see it through in the dark green light shed from C. E. Kempe's very eighteen-ninety glass. The chapel generally has a rather decayed appearance, especially the Baylie Chapel on the north side which was unluckily "improved" in 1890. Such a state of things is sad as this chapel is a holy place indeed. Under the altar are the remains of Sir Thomas White, the London Merchant Taylor who founded the college in 1555, Archbishop Juxon (1582–1663), who attended Charles I at the scaffold, and Arch-

bishop Laud (1573–1645), whose culture, taste for art, and piety pervade the college and whose ghost walks, truncated, down the library.

It is wrong to proceed further in exploring St. John's College without paying tribute to the munificence and taste of that great high churchman Laud. He was responsible for the superb second quad, approached through a slimly-vaulted passage. The Colonnades of the Tuscan order, wrongly attributed to Inigo Jones, stretch along two sides. Notice how light this quadrangle is, because the buildings surrounding it are well proportioned. The statues of Charles I and his Queen, over the colonnades, are by Le Sueur, who did the equestrian statue of Charles I at Charing Cross. I wish I could think the grass laid down in this quadrangle were an improvement.

In Oxford the smallest entrances give on to the greatest wonders. The tiny gate in the middle of the far side of this quadrangle opens into St. John's College Garden. The grass before you, sometimes enlivened by the targets of the Oxford Toxophily Club, and always by the carefully planted groups of trees, are the work of the two greatest exponents of romantic landscape gardening, Capability Brown and Humphrey Repton. An immense sense of space has been created by these eighteenth century planners in a comparatively small area. On the left is a rock garden, not in keeping with the rest of the lay-out, but excellent in itself. Walk down the long stretch of grass before you for fifty yards and then turn back to see the garden front of Laud's buildings. The long, low line of the parapeted front, the judiciously placed windows excite the admiration of classic-and romantic-minded people alike. "From the gardens—where for so many summers the beauty of England has rested in the shadow of the chestnut trees, amid the music of the chimes, and in the air heavy with the scent of the acacia flowers—from the gardens, Laud's building looks rather like a country house than a college." *Andrew Lang.*

The library runs round the upper storey of the colonnade quadrangle. There is a coloured bust of Laud. A portrait of Charles I is said to have "the whole Book of Psalms written in the lines of the face and on the hairs of the head, which may be read with the assistance of a good magnifying glass".* Some sumptuous vestments belonging to Laud are still preserved in a press here.

The Senior Common Room has a plaster Renaissance ceiling by Roberts who did the older part of the ceiling in the Library of Queen's College.

There are some Gothic Revival buildings (1880–1901) along the St. Giles' Front to the north, executed by a son of Sir Gilbert Scott, in a style at once more original and seemly than that of his father.

P E O P L E .   Edmund Campion (1540–1581). Fellow. Martyred. His name perpetuated by Campion Hall (q.v.).

Archbishop Laud (1573–1645) *vide supra*. President. Had a play performed to James I by the college which caused the king to fall asleep. Revised the University Statutes. A judicious university officeholder. A generous patron. Prohibited the playing of football. Suspected of Romanism. It was, for a time, thought "'scandalous' to give him the usual courteous greetings in the street or college quadrangle". Laud helped to start the reputation for High Churchmanship which Oxford has enjoyed ever since. Beheaded.

* *The Oxford University and City Guide* 1810.

Archbishop Juxon (1582–1663) *vide, supra*. President. Benefactor to the college. Survived the Commonwealth.

James Shirley (1596–1666), Dramatist.

Admiral Van Tromp when entertained at this college got so drunk that he had to be taken home in a wheelbarrow.

Rev. Henry Longueville Mansel (1820–1871), High churchman, who wished that he might see "all the German critics at the bottom of the German Ocean".*

Dr. James, the late president of this college, was a great philatelist. It is said that an undergraduate went to call on the president in his room and found two gentlemen on the floor sticking stamps into an enormous album. One was the president, the other was another great philatelist, King George V.

St. John's, always conservative, had no married Fellows "till at least 1898".†

Keble College.

B U I L D I N G S , 1870–1878. Sole architect, W. Butterfield (1814–1900), also architect of Balliol Chapel, All Saint's,

Margaret Street, London; St. Alban's, Holborn, London; Rugby School, Merton College new buildings (since defaced) and many other works.

* Quoted by Gribble in *The Romance of Oxford Colleges*.
† Falconer Madan, *Oxford Outside the Guide Books*.

Jonah and the Whale by Abraham Van Linge. Typical Oxford
seventeenth century glass in Lincoln Chapel.

The Colonnade (1733), New Buildings, Magdalen College.

It is unfortunate that William Butterfield, next to Bodley and George Gilbert Scott (son of Sir Gilbert), the greatest exponent of the Gothic Revival, should have paid so little regard to the texture and colour of Oxford stone in this, his largest work in Oxford. As an essay in the right arrangement of masses, in good proportion and originality in the Gothic manner, Keble College is by far the best Gothic Revival work in either Oxford or Cambridge. One has only to compare the way Butterfield treats by varied arrangement of windows and projecting blocks, what might otherwise be a dull wall along the road opposite the parks, with, let us say, the over-bearing, front of New College in Holywell by Sir Gilbert Scott and others, to realize how admirable an architect Butterfield is. One has only to stand in Keble main quad when a sunset has drained the colour from the bricks, to see how admirably the chapel and hall and surrounding buildings are proportioned to the sunk expanse of the quad. It is only when a bright sun throws up the uncompromising colour of the brickwork with its various skilful but unlovely patterns, that Butterfield appears at his worst. Keble College is a whole scheme which hangs together, the chapel dominating everything as it should in a college which was founded "for perpetuating academic education definitely based upon the Church of England". Whatever criticisms admirers of the Renaissance may level against Keble College, they cannot say that it is a copy of anything. It is not the product of an antiquarian but of an architect. Sir Gilbert Scott, whose work is all too prominent in Oxford and England, was a copyist. Butterfield was an inventor.

The chapel (1876) does not appear so vast within as it would lead one to believe it is from without. This is because it has the fault of revealing all of itself at once. The general effect of wriggling pews, shining brass, mosaics, brickwork, variegated vaulting and soaring marble is indeed overwhelming. The huge white cross on the altar, so daring a thing to introduce as a permanent fixture in the 'seventies, arrests the attention.

In a sort of transept called Dean Liddon Chapel is Holman Hunt's *Light of the World*, which may be seen on request. Holman Hunt is said to have been so angry at Keble College charging an admission fee of 6d. to see his picture, that he painted the replica which now hangs in St. Paul's Cathedral.

The hall and library contain many Butterfield fittings and Richmond's excellent portrait of Keble himself, to whose memory the college was built as a result of subscription among Tractarians.

The planning of Keble differs from older colleges in that the rooms give on to passages. In older colleges, each side of a quadrangle has a series of staircases unconnected by passages, so that the quadrangles are virtually squares, with numerous separate houses.

Keble College was opened in 1870. There are no Fellows. The dons are Tutors only. The annual revenue from endowments of the foundation is £500. The lowest revenue anywhere else is at Hertford (£11,200).

Lady Margaret Hall.

Lady Margaret Hall is away in North Oxford by the banks of the Cherwell. It contains about 150 women students who are expected to read for the Honours School. "Each student has a room which serves as a sitting-room and bedroom."

BUILDINGS. The buildings are in various styles of pre-war Renaissance, the date 1910 and the French Renaissance of Sir Reginald Blomfield in red brick and stone prevailing. To set off this conglomeration, Sir Giles Gilbert Scott has designed a slightly renaissance collection of buildings, the most satisfactory of his designs in Oxford, and a cruciform Byzantine-Romanesque chapel, whose interior has a pretty effect as a whole but whose detail is not so satisfactory.

Lincoln College.

BUILDINGS. The two quadrangles which compose most of this little college are ancient, not improved by nineteenth century battlements. Neither the hall, ancient

and over-restored, nor the New Library (1906–1907) are worth seeing, though the latter is interesting to bibliophiles. But the chapel (1631) is the most perfect seventeenth century one in Oxford and worth the trouble of asking for the key at the porter's lodge. One's first impression is that the chapel is "high" (which it is not) and that incense is used. But this is the scent of the cedar-wood. When one's eyes get used to the dim light the magnificence of this seventeenth century woodwork and the huge classic screen become apparent. Then one sees the glass, by Abraham Van Linge (the younger), a Dutchman who did much glass in Oxford

which has been destroyed in favour of Burne-Jones and worse. Every window is full of seventeenth century glass and the east window is the best of all, particularly the light showing Jonah and the whale.

PEOPLE.
Sir William Davenant (1606–1668), Poet.

Dr. John Radcliffe (1650–1714), Fellow, Physician; one of Oxford's greatest benefactors, gave the Radcliffe Camera, the Radcliffe Observatory and Infirmary. Offended Queen Anne by styling her infirmity "nothing but the vapours". (D.N.B.). See Radcliffe Camera.

John Wesley (1703–1791), Fellow, to whom a little bust has lately been fixed up in the front quadrangle. He was always a methodical man. "Mondays and Tuesdays was allotted for the classics; Wednesdays to logic and ethics; Thursdays, to Hebrew and Arabic; Fridays, to metaphysics and natural philosophy; Saturdays, to oratory and poetry, but chiefly to composition in these arts; and the Sabbath to divinity."* He founded the "Holy Club"—a rare project for eighteenth century Oxford—for regular living and frequent partaking of the Sacrament. Its members included the Rev. James Harvey (of Lincoln), author of *Meditations among the Tombs*, Charles Wesley (of Ch: Ch:) and George Whitefield (of Pembroke). Many years later J. Wesley met Beau Nash (of Jesus) in Bath on a narrow pavement. Nash is said to have said "I never make way for a fool" and stood his ground. "Don't you? I always do", replied Wesley, stepping aside.†

Robert Montgomery (1807–1855), the Moravian poet, not so feeble as Macaulay made him out to be.

* Southey's *Life of Wesley*.
† Quoted by Francis Gribble in *The Romances of Oxford Colleges*.

Edward Tatham (1749–1834), Fellow and rector. A fine eccentric, fiercely opposed the examination system with far-sighted sensible arguments: though Rector preferred to live in the country and lost the key of the college.

Mark Pattison (1813–1884), Rector, not without a struggle and his autobiography should be read for its self-revelation and its exposition of the hatreds of academic life.

Magdalen College.

BUILDINGS. Magdalen College Tower (1492–1507) dominates the buildings. It is seen at its best from the banks of the Cherwell in the Botanic Garden with Mag-

dalen Bridge (by John Gwynn, R.A., in 1779, and widened 1882–1883) acting as a plinth. Oddly enough the tower looks top heavy from the High Street or from the bridge itself, appearing to taper downwards in diminishing stages.

Magdalen, though a "show college", presents an untidy and scattered appearance from the High Street. The lodge is set at an awkward angle to the entrance quad, a useless and dull Gothic Revival gate (Bodley, 1884) stands beside it and some of Bodley's least successful work (1882–1884) called St. Swithin's is set parallel with the High Street. Here the rooms, besides letting in the full roar of the traffic, are so placed that the natural approach to

Magdalen, along the trim grass sward in front of the Bodley Buildings, is partly built up. The singularly ugly tracery in the large west window (mid-seventeenth century) of the chapel is all the more emphasized by this arrangement. It cannot have been so noticeable when Inigo Jones' gateway (of which there are remains in the Tower) stood in front of it, flanked by a parapeted wall. A. W. Pugin built yet another gateway (destroyed by Bodley) in its place in 1836.

By far the most successful building on the long High Street front of Magdalen (excepting the Tower) is what is now the college library. This handsome hall in the Perpendicular manner was built by J. C. Buckler (see Jesus College) in 1851 as a schoolroom for Magdalen College School (now housed across the river). This hall, at the corner of Long Wall Street and the High, is one of the best pieces of Gothic Revival in Oxford. Though Mr. Buckler lacked the intrepidity of Butterfield, he built in a manner at once original and harmonious, which is more than can be said for any other Gothic Revival work in the University, excepting perhaps Pusey House.

The quaint building which confronts one at the entrance to Magdalen is called the Grammar Hall (fifteenth century) and is all that remains of old Magdalen Hall, mostly burned down in 1820. It is the subject of numberless etchings and sketches and water colours, partly, I suspect, because it is easy to draw. Also in this odd-shaped space are the President's Lodgings (unmistakably Bodley and very yellow), a pretty little open-air pulpit, and a war memorial of the usual sort.

The chapel is approached under the arch and on the right. It is unnecessarily dark owing to there being too much stained glass. The Victorian windows should be removed and clear glass should take the place of the smaller enamelled windows, which in turn should be moved from the ante-chapel back to the choir where they were originally. One would then see once more the superb organ screen by L. N. Cottingham, who restored the chapel (1829–1834) in its present delicate Georgian-Perpendicular manner. The west window looks well from within. It is a copy in chiaro-scuro by Richard Greenbury, painter to Lord Arundel, of a painting by Christopher Schwartz, the sixteenth century artist of Munich who was at one time in the school of Titian. It was liberally touched up by Francis Eginton, the transparency artist of Handsworth, in 1794. The other windows in the ante-chapel were introduced by a Laudian President named Accepted Frewen.

After the chapel come the cloisters. One misses the arched roof and superb proportion of the cloisters at New College. The figures on the buttresses are odd and a pair, who may be described as dancing, are the wonder of visitors.

The hall with a large "Oriel" window, a Jacobean screen, linenfold panelling and a Bodley roof has an excellent portrait of Prince Rupert by Michael Wright (1672) and other pictures, mostly copies. From the cloisters below the steps up to the hall may be obtained a good view of the Founder's Tower (late fifteenth century), across the grass enclosure. This is a happy piece of architecture and contains a royal suite once inhabited by Edward VIII when Prince of Wales. The view of the hall and chapel with the bell tower at an odd angle behind them, as viewed from the north side of the cloisters is curiously two dimensional. Two narrow tunnels lead out into the finest part of the college. This is a great grass space bounded on the west by a small eighteenth century deer park, to the north by a long handsome eighteenth century block called New Buildings (begun in 1733 from the designs of Edward Holdsworth, Fellow). On the east are the walks entered between flower beds, the path on the college side being called Addison's Walk. If you turn to the right as you enter them you will come to a somewhat squalid block of buildings by the bridge and looking over the river. Here Oscar Wilde is said to have had his rooms.

It is worth while going right up to New Buildings and standing in the magnificent colonnade running with vaulted plaster ceiling the whole length of the block. Notice the eighteenth century numbers over each staircase, gold on black. The ground floor rooms look on to the deer park which curls round the back. It was once a custom from these windows to try to make the deer drunk by giving them pieces of sugar soaked in port.

New Buildings are only part of a scheme. The original idea was to make a three-sided quadrangle in this style facing the water meadows and walks, pulling down the north side of the cloisters. A later scheme for Gothicizing the buildings in the 1805 manner by Humphrey Repton also came to nothing. One must regret, however, that the college authorities, when they added more buildings a few years ago, let Sir Giles Gilbert Scott continue Bodley's feeble Gothic Revival work in St. Swithin's, rather than erect a block at right-angles to the present New Buildings, after the designs of the talented Holdsworth.

PEOPLE. Magdalen is the richest college, for its size, with an income of £102,500.

It recently spent some of its money in building up a wall on the St. Clement's boundary of its property and pulling it down again. It is a matter for regret that the money was not spent in saving neighbouring land from the speculative builder.

William Grocyn (1446?–1519), Greek scholar.

John Colet (1467?–1519), Dean of St. Paul's, school founder.

John Lyly (1554?–1606), Dramatist. "Neglected his studies."

Reginald Pole (1500–1558), Cardinal and last R.C. Archbishop of Canterbury.

Thomas Wolsey (1475?–1530), Cardinal.

Richard Foxe (?) (1448?–1528), Bishop. See Corpus Christi.

John Hampden (1594–1643), Puritan.

George Wither (1588–1667), Puritan poet.

Rev. Henry Sacheverell (1674?–1724), Tory politician and high church preacher.

Joseph Addison (1672–1719), Essayist. "Of nervous habits." "Kept late hours."

William Collins (1721–1759), Poet.

Edward Gibbon (1737–1794), Historian. "The fellows, or monks, of my time were decent men who supinely enjoyed the gifts of the founder." Described in *Autobiography* his fourteen month's residence as "the most idle and unprofitable of my whole life". Sent down.

Rev. James Hurdis (1763–1801), Pleasant pastoral poet in the manner of his friend Cowper. Made feeble vindication of Magdalen against Gibbon's attack.

Rev. Martin Joseph Routh (1755–1854), President 1791–1854. Preferred to travel to London by coach. High churchman. A character and link with the past.

Charles Reade (1814–1884), Novelist. Lived in a room, ground floor, No. 2 New Buildings, surrounded by looking glass. "Thought so highly of the college cook that, when in London, he often had his dinner cooked at Magdalen and sent up to town in a set of silver dishes."* When Dean wore a bright green coat with brass buttons.

John Conington (1825–1869), Professor of Latin. Known as "the sick vulture".

John Addington Symonds (1840–1893), Fellow 1862.

Oscar O'Flahertie Wills Wilde (1856–1900). Rooms overlooking river decorated with fans and blue china. "On one occasion eight stalwart Philistines bound him with ropes and trailed him along the ground to the top of a hill. Instead of losing his temper, he expressed himself as lost in admiration of the view."†

Sir Herbert Warren (1853–1930), President and poet.

Manchester College.

Manchester College was opened in 1893. It is a Unitarian theological college from Manchester, was designed by Manchester architects and looks like a bit of Manchester translated into Oxford stone. Northern manufacturers are well known for their partiality for the Pre-Raphaelites, so that it is not surprising to

* Francis Gribble, *The Romance of Oxford Colleges.*
† Francis Gribble, *ibid.*

find the windows filled with glass by Burne Jones executed by William Morris. Great as the Pre-Raphaelites were, stained glass was not their strong point and the windows of Manchester Chapel shed a green light on carved but, of course, uncoloured wood-work.

Mansfield College.

Mansfield College was opened in 1889. It is a Congregational Theological College and nearer North Oxford than its neighbour Manchester College. It is the most successful work in Oxford of its architect, Mr. Basil Champneys. The Perpendicular buildings, here and there hung with wistaria, form an excellent group, spaciously laid out round a wide grass space.

THE MARKET, a covered collection of shops between the High Street and Market Street, was designed by John Gwynn in 1771. He was the architect of Magdalen Bridge. There seem to be mostly fishmongers, butchers and greengrocers. Though none of the old shop fronts remain, and though the colonnade has gone, the market has a Georgian air and one somehow feels that the things one buys here must be better than those displayed in the more flashy shops of the main streets. Once a year two Clerks of the Market are sworn in at the first meeting of Congregation in the Michaelmas Term. " . . . diligenter ea curabitis . . . quae ad officium Clericorum Mercatus aliqua ratione vel pertinent, vel pertinere possunt." For this they receive £5 a year and are invited to the annual corn-rent dinner by the Estate Bursars of the colleges. At this dinner they announce the current price of corn in Oxford Market. Their office is the last relic (except for the mysterious Delegates of Privileges) of the control the University once had over the town.

THE MARTYR's MEMORIAL (1841) It is one of the early successes of Gilbert Scott. It was done while he was still in partnership with W. B. Moffat and winning competitions for building workhouses. It is a copy of an "Eleanor Cross" with sculptured figures of Cranmer, Latimer and Ridley (who were burned, opposite Balliol, for Protestant beliefs in 1541) by Henry Weekes in the manner of Chantrey at his worst. It is a well proportioned thing and compares favourably with the skimpy war memorial at the other end of St. Giles. A chamber pot is put on top of the Martyrs Memorial by practical jokers, with almost irritating regularity.

Fervent undergraduates preach here on warm evenings.

ST. MARY MAGDALENE CHURCH, between Balliol and Elliston and Cavell's is broad in appearance, High liturgically and Low by association since the north aisle was added in 1841 to commemorate the Oxford martyrs. Its south aisle has decorated work of some interest to archaeologists, but the church was so thoroughly restored within and without in the 'nineties and earlier that it is now visited chiefly as a place of worship.

ST. MARY THE VIRGIN CHURCH. The building is frequently mistaken for the Cathedral. Its spire and many pinnacles (restored by J. C. Buckler, 1861, and the spire almost entirely rebuilt by Sir Thomas Jackson, 1897–1898) are the most prominent feature of the High Street. The entrance porch was erected in 1637, the

ST. MARY MAGDALENE FROM ST. GILES'

most baroque construction in Oxford. Archbishop Laud got into considerable trouble from Puritans for causing the statue of the Virgin and Holy Child to be placed in the niche. Notice the wrought iron gates.

The interior has lost its character since many of the excellent box-pews, designed by Thomas Plowman from 1826–1828, were removed in the recent "restoration" by Sir Charles Nicholson. What Sir Charles has substituted lacks character. The stained glass is all too prominent and none too lovely. The west window by Kempe (1891) is to Dean Burgon, author of the well known line in a prize poem, "A rose-red city half as old as time" (see Worcester College).

The N.E. corner of the church is the oldest part (1320), but little of the old work remains. The nave was finished in 1498. The chancel (1462) is the loveliest part of the church, superbly proportioned and spared Victorian and modern stained glass. Amy Robsart is buried in the church, and Dr. John Radcliffe. Among the many excellent monuments remaining, notice the Farmor one in Batty Langley Gothick executed by F. Townesend of Oxford in 1762 in the tower, and the Holoway Monument by Stanton in the choir. Above the altar (unfortunate blue hangings) some old niches have excellent modern statues by Mr. Burton. Adam de Brome (d. 1322) is buried under an altar tomb to the west of the intersection of the tower. He founded Oriel College.

Rev. John Henry Newman was vicar

here 1828–1843 and crowded the church out.

The University sermon is preached here on Sundays at 10.30 a.m. during Full Term and at the Assizes. The Proctors and Vice-Chancellor are obliged to attend. The preacher wears a black gown. A Latin Litany is said and a Latin sermon is preached once a year.

HISTORY AND PEOPLE. The N.E. corner of this church is the heart of the University. Hence the present organization spread out. In this corner was originally a two storey building.

From the fourteenth to the seventeenth centuries it was the original Convocation House. It was also used upstairs, as the University Library from the fourteenth to the fifteenth century. Then it was the archive room till the seventeenth century. Since then it has been a powder magazine for the Civil War, a type-store, a book-seller's storeroom, a grammar school, a fire station, a law lecture room, a chapel, a parish room, a chapel. St. Mary's has long been "the University Church". (All Saints is now called "the City Church" and here the Mayor and Corporation go for service.)

In Catholic days "the various chapels of St. Mary's were assigned to the different Faculties for their deliberations, and the Congregation of all the Faculties, Regents (i.e., teachers) and non-Regents alike, met in the choir, forming the supreme governing body of the University".*

Various awe-inspiring scenes have occurred here.

Cranmer in 1555 was placed on a low platform opposite the pulpit to have a sermon preached against him after his trial.

Queen Elizabeth made a speech in Latin

* Dr. J. Wells. *Oxford and its Colleges.*

after listening for three days to learned disputes here.

Dr. Sacheverell preached here.

Rev. John Wesley preached here.

Rev. John Keble started the Oxford Movement here with his sermon on "National Apostasy" (1833).

Merton College.

BUILDINGS. A series of higgledy piggledy ancient buildings, set among meadows and brooded over by the firm pinnacled tower of what is now the chapel, make up the greater part of the college.

Besides these is a building by Butterfield (1864), once original but never beautiful, which has been remodelled (1930) so that it is now not even original. There is also a quadrangle in an elaborate 1905 Anglo-Jackson manner, though the architect is the ubiquitous Mr. Basil Champneys. The Warden's Lodgings on the other side of the street is in a similar style. The hall is mostly Gilbert Scott (1872).

The two buildings to see in Merton are the library and the chapel, and of these I give preference to the library. It was built in 1377 and is the oldest of the college libraries. It takes up two sides of "Mob Quad", occupying the upper storey. Though there is a certain amount of sixteenth and seventeenth century work in the woodwork, roof and walls, the appearance of this library is still fifteenth century or earlier. Dim light, shut in silence (save, of course,

Hawksmoor's Cupola (1736) on the High Street front of the Queen's College.

The Radcliffe Observatory, now a science laboratory. In the foreground on the right is a new wing of the Radcliffe Infirmary.
The Observatory was designed by Henry Keene from 1772–76,
and was finished by James Wyatt in 1795.

for aeroplanes), horse-boxes, vellum and leather and a smell of old wood. The library should certainly be seen. It conveys better than anywhere else an impression of ancient Oxford.

A Victorian barrister turned minor poet describes the light pouring in a tranquil flood into Merton Chapel "On marble chequered floor and desk of brass". Brass, marble, Victorian fittings of the tawdriest sort, wasted space and unsatisfactory proportions for so noble and imposing an exterior do indeed make up one's first impression of the inside of Merton Chapel. The transepts are fourteenth and fifteenth century. The tower was finished in 1450.

The choir is late thirteenth century ("Decorated") and it contains an unforgettable collection of thirteenth century glass in all the windows. Notice how the light does not pour in colours on to the floor but is merely dimmed daylight. This is a distinguishing quality of mediaeval glass from later work. The east window, two years ago, was deprived of some excellent enamelled glass (W. Price, 1702) because it was "not in keeping". I do not know what has happened to it. There are fifteenth century brasses and a mid-fifteenth century brass lectern.

The shady gardens have an eighteenth century summer house and a good outlook over the meadows.

PEOPLE. Merton is the oldest college in Oxford or Cambridge. It was founded in 1264. What Balliol was to the nineteenth century, Merton was to the fourteenth. The names do not convey as much as those Balliol Victorians, but Mr. Falconer Madan* gives a beautiful list: "Walter Burley (the Doctor Perspicuus), Thomas

* Oxford Outside the Guide Books.

Bradwardine (the Doctor Profundus), John Dumbleton, Richard Swinshed, William Merle (the founder of scientific meteorology), John of Gaddesden, Simon Bredon and John Ashenden were names to conjure with: six archbishops of Canterbury of that century were Mertonians. John Wycliffe was probably a Fellow."

Rev. John Jewel (1522–1571), Bishop of Salisbury, early Protestant, removed to Corpus.

Sir Thomas Bodley (1545–1613), Fellow.

Sir Henry Savile (1549–1622), Fellow. Scholar.

William Harvey (1578–1657), Warden for one year in place of a Puritan. Discovered the circulation of the Blood.

Jasper Heywood (1535–1598), Jesuit and poet.

Anthony Wood (1632–1695), Antiquary. Wrote on Oxford and is the source of the lively and scandalous stories of seventeenth century life in the University. Objected to Warden Clayton, who brought his wife to the college. She ordered a looking glass "for her to see her ugly face and body to the middle and perhaps lower".

Merton started its reputation for gaiety at the time of the Civil Wars. When Charles I removed to Oxford, his queen, Henrietta Maria, held her court at Merton where she lodged. Merton Gardens became a walk for the tired Royalist soldiers to meet their ladies. Three more Royal visits to Merton followed the Civil Wars—Charles II paid two, and James II paid one. The college became rich and smart. The gardens became notorious. Sir Richard Steele (1672–1729) seems to have been the last well-known member of Merton until the nineteenth century when Hartley

THE LIBRARY, MERTON COLLEGE

Coleridge, a few bishops and Lord Randolph Churchill came from the college. But even the embryo-Bishops seem to have been gay. Francis Gribble* quotes a story about Dr. Mandell Creighton (1843–1901), later Bishop of London, being employed as an undergraduate "to fetch in after dinner a supply of penny whistles and other musical instruments, armed with which, with tea trays as drums, making the most horrible din, and letting off squibs and crackers as they went, the undergraduates marched round and round the Fellows' quad". The spirit of the Restoration still survives, I like to think, in Merton. The gardens were used for a famous sham duel in the nineteen-twenties, at this time too the Merton "Smokers' Concerts" were famous.

* *The Romance of the Oxford Colleges.*

Many Oxford people will regret the retirement of Thomas Bowman, the late warden, one of the last characters among Oxford dons.

MESOPOTAMIA is the name given to a walk along the Cherwell between the parks and St. Clements. At one point along the walk the last view of Oxford's towers and spires may be obtained, as one sees it in the old engravings—Cotswold stone above meadows, without a modern house in view.

ST. MICHAEL'S CHURCH in the Corn Market has what is either a very early Norman or late Saxon tower. It served as a watch tower. Since it is so old, no one will pull it down and it holds its own against the commercial "improvements" of the Corn. The church inside was so puritanically "restored" by G. E. Street in 1855 as to be dull. The high pitched Saxon proportions have been allowed to remain. There are a few charming fragments of mediaeval glass.

MORRIS WORKS, THE. The place might be a cathedral. The reverence of the guides who conduct parties of motor-worshippers is no different from that of licensed guides on holy ground. Facts, figures, jokes. A story here, a demonstration there, a certain effect, a certain gasp of wonder from the worshippers at the sight of the engine dropping into its place on the belt, a pleasure for the guide every time. And at the leather cutting bench "This machine is capable of doing 1,000 revolutions a second". How little different from "And this masonry is said to be 1,000 years old". The romance of history, the romance of industry.

It would not be possible to see over the whole of the Morris Works in three days. I spent little more than an hour for the purposes of this book. I should have spent more. But I am so literary, so fearful of machinery, such an escapist, that a few minutes more would have sent me off my rocker.

You will have to be content with my impressions.

William R. Morris started as a bicycle repairer in James Street before the war; thirty years ago he fixed the back-pedalling brakes and mended punctures for undergraduates. He also ran a garage, a cheerful little affair, something like a green house, wedged in beside a bastion of the old city wall. In 1914 he produced a round-nosed eight horse-power motor-car.

It is not for me to trace the development of the Morris industry to the ninety acres of good agricultural land which are now covered by its Cowley factories. You will find plenty about that in pamphlets obtainable at the Morris works. It is not for me to write up the character of Lord Nuffield. But it has always occurred to me that the great black wall of the University has shadowed his life. He has stormed it and won. Oxford is no longer primarily a University town, but primarily an industrial town. The shade of the wall may now seem grateful to Lord Nuffield. He is able to bolster its crumbling bastions, to mortice it with gold. And many of the men who help to make the gold have never set foot inside one of the colleges; their lives are spent walking along beside the belt, screwing in a nut and bicycling home to some new-built already-forgotten building estate near the works.

To one who, like me, sees nothing short of horror in such a life, the Morris Works are an inferno, the houses round them a warning to the rest of England against the speculative builder. But I am behind the time. The men are well paid. The more they work, the more money they can get. Each workman is a shareholder and though, when he gets the sack, he does not take his shares with him, it is to his interest to work his hardest so that his shares pay a good dividend. Money is the inducement to the men to work as it was, alas, the inducement to me to write this book.

But picture to yourself the life of a man who works, let us say, on part of the assembling of the Morris Eight—the Morris cars are only assembled at their Oxford works, the engines are made in Coventry, the radiators in North Oxford, the body-work at the Pressed Steel Co., opposite the

Oxford Works—picture to yourself the life of this man. When he first comes to the works he sees a moving belt. That moving belt is to govern his life. It is fourteen and three-quarter miles long. It crawls all over those neat north-lighted airy engineering halls, picking up more and more pieces of the Morris car until finally it has collected the whole lot together, ready for a test drive along the road to Garsington.

The belt does not move very fast. A child can toddle faster. It gives the man four minutes to do the job he is selected to do. Let us say he has to screw four important nuts on to a part of the car. The belt is below him. He has to bend down to his work. At the Ford factory, the belt is at eye level so that a man may work standing up. But men are said to see better looking at things from above than at head level. The Morris authorities claim that a fraction above ground level ensures more thorough work than a belt at eye level.

A man arrives at the factory at eight o'clock. He takes his position at the moving belt. He screws on loosely the first four nuts of the day. Further down the line is another man who tightens up his four nuts. By thus splitting the job into two, the work is more certain to be thorough. If the first has left out a nut by mistake, the second further down the line can make good the defect. All the time a man is working, the belt is slowly moving along. Five hundred cars come out of the works in a day. The number may be increased to 628. But then the belt moves faster. If one gang wants to produce more cars, and so make more money for the men on it, it has only to agree among its members to work faster, and the increased output and higher wages will be forthcoming.

A man has, normally, four minutes in which to screw on his nuts, following along the belt all the time. But he can finish his job in three and a half minutes and stand up and straighten his back for half-a-minute. While he does so, everything will seem to move in the opposite direction. The belt governs his life. It provides an interesting problem for the students of time.

At twelve o'clock there is an hour off for lunch. At one, work again until five o'clock. Then the men bicycle away, six abreast, to the villa, the bird bath, the wireless, the garden and a bi-weekly visit to the pictures.

I have painted an unnecessarily gloomy picture. The men can smoke at work. Each has good wages. Each can be fairly sure of promotion. Each can change his job. Each genuinely likes motor-cars.

To what end is this endeavour? That a commercial traveller may take his girl down a side turning in this model, that an undergraduate may kill himself in that, that a doctor may save someone from death in a third, that the country lanes may be tarred and the houses spread out and out and out.

Picture to yourself another scene. Miss Angle is reading "English" in the Bodleian Library. The Gutnish and High Finnish dialects puzzle her poor head and dance about beneath her spectacles. When she was a little baby, the pride of Bob Angle's home in 14 Stipendiary Street, Macclesfield, little did they think their weak-eyed lamb would one day read Gutnish in the Bodleian. Bob and Martha Angle saved their money that their daughter might escape from industrialism. They did not put it like that. They wanted her to better herself. She bettered herself more than they expected. She got a scholarship in "English" to Oxford from the country school. Now she is reading Gutnish. The bells call out from New College Tower and

St. Mary's. Five o'clock. Miss Angle must bike back to St. Hugh's, repeating the i-mutations to herself as she sails down Banbury Road.

To what end is her endeavour? An unspectacular second and a job teaching in a school, all her enthusiasm for English killed by Gutnish, her native sincerity covered by an Oxford University veneer which may easily turn to bitterness. And she will teach girls who are either to work in the mills or else to get scholarships to enable them to read Gutnish.

If this is learning on the one side and the belt is industry on the other, do you wonder that Lord Nuffield founds a college for enquiring into the relations between industry and learned studies? Lord Nuffield's position must be terrifying. The responsibility for so strange a way of using human life must weigh on him. The awed devotion which every Oxford citizen feels for the University impels him to make enquiries. What is it they are at? Can those dons teach us to use our leisure profitably?

And for the don, little effort comes from his side. Few undergraduates and fewer dons have been over the Morris Works at Cowley. A visitor from the University will see the aesthetic beauty of the machinery. He may even venture to the finest sight of all, the pressed steel factory where the whole chassis of a car is stamped out of the metal—where, if you got your wrist watch under the presses, it would squash out with a face as large as a grandfather's clock. Very impressive no doubt. But remote from Gutnish.

Between Morris Cowley and the Bodleian there is a great gulf. Those on either side of it have nothing in common but flesh and blood.

Certainly every tutor should make a compulsory tour with his pupils of the Morris Works once a term. It would give them "poise", a "poise" a little steadier than our toppling Oxford poise. If they had visited the works the week I did, they would have seen near a passage where "Beware of Falling Tyres" gives its warning, an advertisement for the O.U.D.S. production of *Much Ado About Nothing*.

Back in the University they would see even larger bills with the same words *Much Ado About Nothing*.

THE MUSIC ROOM in Holywell is a plain stone edifice, like an early Congregational church without, plain and serviceable within. It was opened in 1748 and is the earliest building to be dedicated solely to music in Europe. Handel's Oratorio of Esther was performed for the opening. Since then countless well-known composers have performed there. Probably the strangest performance was given in the 'twenties of this century when Thomas Driberg surprised the usual North Oxford audience by a recital of his poems through a megaphone to an accompaniment of typewriters. The climax was the loud flushing of a lavatory which is near enough to the platform to be audible to an audience.

New College.

BUILDINGS. Of the Gothic sights of Oxford, New College Cloisters and Chapel are among the best. The rest of this college, except the gardens, is not so good.

The pleasantest approach is from New College Lane, where the mediaeval entrance lodge remains, shut in among the high stone walls.

The gardens are straight ahead across the now ill-proportioned first quadrangle. The

157

entrance gates and railings are of beautiful wrought-ironwork (presumably late seventeenth century). They are said to come from Canon's Park, Edgware. The gardens are laid out in the Georgian landscape manner with lawn and carefully disposed trees.

The old city wall (thirteenth century) bounds most sides and the elms of Magdalen deer park tower behind it. Against this wall, on the other side, Lord Nuffield had his garage.

The chapel (c. 1400) on the left of the lodge is on the usual T-shaped plan. The ante-chapel makes one catch one's breath.

"Where the tall shafts, that mount in massy pride,
Their mingling branches shoot from side to side."*

After the noble proportions of this building, Oxford's nearest approach in beauty to King's College Chapel, Cambridge, comes the realization of the excellence of the glass. The transept windows are filled with fourteenth century stained glass described by Dr. Wells† as the finest in Oxford.

The choir has fascinating windows on the south door side enamelled by William Price in 1740. Notice the semi-Gothic canopies. The windows on the west side of the choir were done in 1765 by William Peckitt. Here there is also enamelling

* Verses on Sir Joshua Reynolds' Painted Window at New College, Oxford. T. Warton the Younger. 1782.
† Oxford and its Colleges.

and an Oriental note is introduced into the decoration of Old Testament figures. Originally one was supposed to turn west in the choir and see, soaring above the organ screen, the great west window begun by Sir Joshua Reynolds in 1777 and executed by Thomas Jervais a year later. The organ was placed in 1790 by Wyatt so as to form a frame to a view of the west window from the choir. The present ungainly case which blocks out the best view of the window is part of a restoration by Sir Gilbert Scott, James Pearson and others in the latter half of the nineteenth century (1872–1894). At this time the woodwork was stupidly scraped of its paint, the reredos filled with laughable sculpture and Wyatt's plaster vaulting replaced by the present choir roof.

The Reynolds window is not stained, but enamelled glass. It is executed in specially prepared transparent enamel paint on plain glass. The most exquisite of the many lovely figures in this window has always seemed to me to be the Shepherd in the top left hand light, a self portrait by Reynolds. The upper and central panel, specially designed to be seen from the choir, contains the Virgin, Christ, Joseph and Angels. " . . . my idea is to paint in the great space in the centre Christ in the Manger, on the Principle that Corregio has done it in the famous Picture called the Notte, making all the light proceed from Christ, these tricks of the art, as the[y] may be called, seem to be more properly adapted to Glass painting than any other kind."*

The recent cleaning has shown up the bad cracks in the glass caused, not by storms, but by former attempts to preserve the glass.

* Letter from Sir Joshua to Rev. John Oglander, 1778. Letters of Sir Joshua Reynolds. Edited by F. W. Hilles, 1929.

NEW COLLEGE CHAPEL, BEFORE NINETEENTH CENTURY RESTORATIONS, SHOWING WYATT'S
1790 DESIGN OF THE ORGAN CASE WHICH FRAMES THE REYNOLDS' WEST WINDOW.
FROM AN AQUATINT ENGRAVING IN ACKERMANN'S HISTORY OF OXFORD

Also in the chapel is a silver gilt Pastoral Staff of the Founder exquisitely enamelled and wrought. His mitre is kept in the Warden's Lodgings. It is worth mentioning here that New College possesses a silver gilt salt cellar, presented in 1493, of a most shapely contour.

West of the chapel is the cloister (c. 1400). This should certainly be seen. It is purely a cloister and not a passage way and has, therefore, a contemplative air. The proportions are excellent. The roof is the original one of English oak which seems able well to withstand insects and time. The disposition of an ilex in the garth is happy. From the cloisters the view of All Souls' Towers and the Camera is superb. Only the Reynolds' window looks poor owing to his tampering with the tracery. The plain bell tower of New College rises out of the city wall. In one corner of this cloister is a charming eighteenth century fire engine belonging to the college.

P E O P L E. New College is never called "New". William of Wykeham founded New College in 1379 as an Oxford branch of his college at Winchester. Wykehamists only were admitted to New College until 1854. Even now there is a large number of men from that school who go out to govern the country in various permanent jobs in the civil service. There is, consequently, a Wykehamical flavour to the list of well-known New College men.

Sir Henry Wotton (1568–1639), Poet and diplomatist.

Rev. Thomas Ken (1637–1711), Bishop and hymnwriter.

Rev. Joseph Warton (1722 – 1800), Poet, editor of Pope, friend of Dr. Johnson.

Rev. William Howley (1766–1848), last Archbishop of Canterbury in the old tradition.

Rev. Sydney Smith (1771–1845), Wit. "Got into debt to buy books".

Lionel Johnson (1867–1902), Poet.

"Ill times may be; she hath no thought of time:
　　She reigns beside the waters yet in pride.
　Rude voices cry: but in her ears the chime
　　Of full sad bells brings back her old spring tide.

Like to a queen in pride of place, she wears
　　The splendour of a crown in Radcliffe's dome.
　Well fare she—well! As perfect beauty fares,
　　And those high places that are beauty's home."

N E W   I N N   H A L L   S T R E E T, running parallel with the Cornmarket and east of it, was once known as the Lane of the Seven Deadly Sinnes. Since those days it has become the centre of the Nonconformist life of Oxford City. The Congregational Church (E.F. Revival) faces it, the Wesley Memorial Church, an ambitious building in the "Early Decorated style" with a spire which dominates the west of Oxford is in the street. The interior is indeed "a smooth seventh-heaven of polished pitch pine". Behind it stands the pretty Grecian exterior of the older chapel (1818). Almost next door to the Wesleyan Church is St. Peter-le-Bailey, the first building in Oxford to be designed by Mr. Basil Champneys. It has always been Evangelical and is now used as a chapel by St.

North Oxford.

The Sheldonian (1664–69) and its unknown bearded guards.

Peter's Hall (founded in 1929), an Evangelical hall for undergraduates. The new buildings of this hall, which stand back, cannot be called successful. They are said to be in a Georgian manner and if red brick with Renaissance dressings in stone are Georgian, then St. Peter's Hall is Georgian —but modern municipal-Georgian. The most handsome building in New Inn Hall Street is "Hannington Hall", which is part of what would have been one of Oxford's best buildings if it had been completed. The present block was built in 1832 for the now extinct New Inn Hall. I am unable to discover the name of the architect. Old St. Peter-le-Bailey Church, a plain and handsome eighteenth century structure, stood once at the corner of this street and George Street. It was pulled down in 1872.

NEW ROAD BAPTIST CHURCH has a simple and pleasant early nineteenth century exterior standing back from the road. The interior has been much altered.

NORTH OXFORD. Yet a few yards from the purple-grey Oxford stone of Wadham to the red gaiety of Keble, a step or two north of spreading St. Giles and North Oxford is upon you. North Oxford is now an inner suburb. There is another North Oxford beyond it of sham Tudor villas and new houses which look like council houses and aren't, of un-metalled lanes with bungalows and a Lady Huntingdon Church, of bye-passes, garages and chain stores, but it is not of that North Oxford, the North Oxford of the Morris Radiator Plant that I propose to treat.

The inner North Oxford is a life in itself a home of married dons, don's widows, retired clergymen, retired dons, preparatory schools, theological seminaries, bicycle sheds, ladies' colleges, tea-parties, perambulators and peace except where the Banbury and Woodstock roads roar past their diversity of buildings.

The twisting side roads are as romantic as their names, Norham Gardens, Canterbury Road, Winchester Road; and above this first part of North Oxford the spire of Street's. St. Philip and St. James'* Church, the heart of North Oxford, whose fanciful hips and ridges surge above the tinkle of tea-cups, above the respectable shopping in North Parade, above the silences of flowered bedrooms where the widows of heads of colleges lie dying, their eyes looking out into a sunset over 1860 crenellations so like John Fulleylove's living paintings or the coloured postcards Alden's used to sell.

After this precious romanticizing, I would like you to look closely at North Oxford, for it enshrines the history of University architecture in Oxford.

The battle of the styles, for instance, with Gothic distinctly in the ascendant may be seen to advantage. You will notice one or two Early Victorian villas in a decent classical style by North Parade, turn eastward and you will be in Park Town. Here Italianate villas, the domestic counterpart of the Ashmolean, flank in wide gardens an avenue that leads to Park Crescent. This crescent, or rather oval, is quite like Bath until you look into its detail and realize the date is more 1860 than 1760. But it is a well proportioned, orderly arrangement with more Italianate, Leamington-like villas beyond and Park Terrace another crescent

* Once the home of Broad Churchism but now on the high side. Fr. Ronald Knox made a famous limerick about its incumbent.
    There once was a man who said: " I
    Am a moderate churchman; for why?
        St. Philip you know,
        Was inclined to be low
    But St. James was excessively high."

beyond that. This tiny neighbourhood of Park Town is all you will see, except for a few single villas, of the classic in North Oxford.

But its influence has reached as far as Keble Road where there is an attempt to make a terrace on the classic principle, though the detail is in the Keble manner.

Now notice the Gothic houses of this 1860 date (architects generally Wilkinson & Moore). Often in white (yellow) brick with Bath stone dressings, they are spacious enough behind their red and green, laburnum-hung railings. Stained glass lights their staircases, large halls give way to larger drawing-rooms, Early English and decorated shafts burst into flower beside plate glass windows, blue slate slides down high pitched gables. Each house learns something from Christ Church Cathedral and the Parks' Museum. Each house repeats it in its special way. Ever changing, never the same. The woodwork of the stairs is varnished and ecclesiastical. The gardens are spacious. The interiors remind one of a clergyhouse. There is something monastic about them, for indeed they were built to house monks set free—they marked the triumph of the University Commission of 1877 when a don was allowed to marry without forfeiting his fellowship.

Less monastic, indeed more domestic altogether, as though to say "the don has settled down to married life" are the red brick and Bath stone houses of the 90's also to be seen in North Oxford. The houses are in the Jacobean style, faintly reminiscent of the Examination Schools and in what is called the Anglo-Jackson manner after Sir Thomas Jackson, a late Victorian architect, who did much Neo-Jacobean in the University City. Typical specimens of Anglo-Jackson houses of this later North Oxford will be found in Bardwell Road, St. Margaret's Road, Polstead Road and Rawlinson Road, while smaller examples exist in Chalfont Road. Thereafter followed other revivals all too familiar, the black and white, the pseudo Queen Anne, the Tudor, the modern, the Cotswold. North Oxford contains a few examples where nursery gardens have been sold up or where the large gardens of some 1870 house has been encroached upon by the speculative builder. Mercifully, the majority of these later revivals are confined to the remoter outskirts where the local authorities are responsible for permitting some of the worst placed and most ill-built "development" in England.

There are three formulae for the observant in North Oxford by the use of which they may tell who lives in which house, regardless of the style in which it is built.

(1) A bicycle shed in the garden and a bright red brick appendage in the Tudor style with stained glass; a large house and an ill-kept garden mean a Theological College or something to do with a school.

(2) Lace curtains in the window, well-kept garden, no bicycle shed, all the windows shut, gas-light, mean a retired clergyman or clergyman's widow.

(3) Dark blue or orange curtains or no curtains at all. A bare table except for a bowl of hyacinths in the ground floor window: all the windows open: tooth-brushes airing on the bathroom window ledge: a bicycle shed for three bicycles: an old Morris outside—all mean a don's house and probably one who takes in senior students as lodgers during term time.

Oriel College.

BUILDINGS. The little bowler-hatted parapets of Oriel College attract attention. The view facing the porch in the front quadrangle (1619–1642) is certainly lovely, a curious blending of Perpendicular and Renaissance, as at Wadham and University Colleges. A good statue of the Virgin and Child stands in a niche above equally good ones of Charles I and Edward II while the

staircase forms a plinth. This staircase, when it was enlivened with flower boxes containing geraniums and when the quad was gravelled, made a famous picture post-card view of some beauty. But the grass craze has spread to Oriel. Badly shaped patches of grass fill the quad, which now looks darker and narrower.

The chapel has a good black and white marble floor, seventeenth century wood-work, well carved communion rails and a large "spider" damaged by silly electric light fittings. Unlovely Victorian glass darkens the chapel. The one good window designed by Dr. John Wall (Fellow, founder of the Worcester China Works) and executed by William Peckitt of York (1767) is in a bad state. It is clearly removed from its original position to a distant corner. The hall was well restored by J. N. Comper in 1911, but the walls have since been washed a nasty yellow colour.

The next quadrangle is well worth enter-ing to view Wyatt's stately Ionic library (1788), a lesson for all in how to give a sense of breadth and grandeur to a small space.

Behind this are the remains of the looked-down-on St. Mary Hall, now part of the college. An elaborate form of Perpendicular

Revival will be found along the west side of this quadrangle (Daniel Robertson, 1835). The individuality of St. Mary Hall still remains in this quad which seems so distant from Oriel and which refuses to be put out of countenance by Mr. Basil Champneys' peculiar Rhodes Building (1911), whose front is so yellow and tricky an affair on the High. The statue of Edward VII on this High Street front is not to be forgotten.

PEOPLE. Dr. John Hunter (1728–1793), Anatomist, was at St. Mary Hall. Those below are Oriel names:

Alexander Barclay (1475?–1552), Poet.

Sir Walter Raleigh (1552?–1618). "Un-der streights for want of money" (Aubrey), when an undergraduate.

Rev. Joseph Butler (1692–1752), Author of the *Analogy*. "Wafted to the see [of Durham] in a cloud of metaphysics in which he remained absorbed." Dis-liked Oxford.

Rev. Gilbert White (1720–1793), of Selborne, Naturalist.

Ever since its foundation Oriel Fellow-ships were "open". In this way it was unique among colleges until the University Reforms of the nineteenth century. Thus at the beginning of that century when "educa-tion" was becoming popular, the Provost of the college at that time over-ruled the old custom of electing friends and relations to Fellowships and went in for brains. Owing to the already open Fellowships, Oriel was thus able to steal a march on the other colleges and obtain the best brains.

The result was theological divisions, since theology was then the pursuit of intellec-tuals. Three schools had their leaders in Oriel "Broad churchmen" (really precur-sors of modern Broad churchmen—theolo-gical liberals), Tractarians and Doubters.

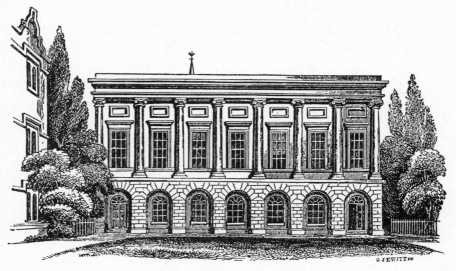

ORIEL COLLEGE LIBRARY, 1788

Broad

Rev. Richard Whately (1787–1863), Archbishop of Dublin. Eccentric. When at tea with a don's wife "An ominous crack was heard; a leg of the chair had given way; he tossed it on to a sofa without comment, and impounded another chair".* Sometimes he lectured lying on a sofa.

Rev. Thomas Arnold (1795–1842), Fellow (came from Corpus Christi). Headmaster of Rugby.

Thomas Hughes (1822–1896), wrote *Tom Brown's Schooldays*. A later product with the point of view of the above.

Tractarians

Rev. John Henry Newman (1801–1890), Fellow (came from Trinity). Cardinal. Only got a "second". Evangelical at first. Occupied Whately's rooms and found a herring

* *Reminiscences of Oxford.* Tuckwell.

hanging there, remnant of Whately's breakfast.

Richard Hurrell Froude (1803–1836), Fellow.

Rev. John Keble (1792–1866), Fellow (came from Corpus Christi).

Rev. Edward Bouverie Pusey (1800–1882), Fellow (from Christ Church whither he returned).

Doubters

Arthur Hugh Clough (1819–1861), Poet, described his time as tutor at Oriel as "bondage in Egypt".

Matthew Arnold (1822–1888), Poet, *Thyrsis* is about Clough. This should be re-read and *The Scholar Gipsy* before an expedition to the country west of Oxford.

Cecil John Rhodes (1853–1902), Imperialist. Obtained a Pass degree. Left £100,000 to Oriel and endowed 170 scholarships at Oxford for Colonials.

164

THE PARKS opposite Keble, are what is, in any other town, called a park. The central space has all the arid level of an athletic ground and here, in season, you may see women playing hockey against men. The athletic grounds are fringed by municipal flower beds and arboreta. The far end of the parks border the Cherwell.

Cherwell! how pleased along thy wil-
    low'd edge
  Erewhile I stray'd, or when the morn
    began
  To tinge aloft the turret's golden fan,
  Or evening glimmer'd o'er the sighing
    sedge!*

Here by the Cherwell is the only really good piece of modern architecture in Oxford, a light footbridge of concrete which humps over the river as airily as a bridge in a Japanese picture. It lacks any ornament but its own grace and a foreground of weeping willow.

ST. PAUL'S CHURCH. The only Greek Revival Church in Oxford. Erected 1835. Architect, H. J. Underwood. The Ionic Portico is particularly effective, viewed as a termination to Gt. Clarendon Street. Interior bare except for much Barocquerie. High.

Pembroke College.

BUILDINGS. Pembroke, behind St. Aldate's Church, is so remote that no one seems to visit it. Its two quadrangles, smothered in ivy, look like some Victorian water colour and one almost expects under-graduates to come out from the Gothic Revival arches wearing mortar boards and gowns and with embryo weepers.

  * *Scenes and Shadows of Days Departed.* Rev. W. L. Bowles, 1837.

The first quadrangle is picturesque in every sense of that word. The second is spacious and the hall (C. Hayward, 1848) is well proportioned within and without. The whole college, except the east, south and west sides of the first quadrangle and the chapel, is early Gothic Revival.

The chapel is a neat Ionic building (1728–1732). When C. E. Kempe, the stained-glass artist, who put in so many hundreds of anaemic green windows into our churches, redecorated this, the chapel of his college, in 1885, he spared the exquisite grey-veined marble altar piece and incorporated it skilfully in his green, red and blue decorations. Pembroke Chapel is far the best decoration by Kempe that I have seen. Only his windows are too heavy and green.

MASTERS' LODGINGS, PEMBROKE COLLEGE

In the first quadrangle some rooms painted about ten years ago in perspective by Mr. John Churchill when an under-graduate, are reverently kept and let to members of the college who will not be supposed to damage them.

I should mention that many of Oxford's best portraits are not in the dining halls of the colleges, but in the private Senior Common Rooms. Pembroke is no exception. The Senior Common Room has three notable portraits, a Reynolds (of Dr. Johnson), an Opie and a Lawrence. Here too is the huge teapot which belonged to Dr. Johnson. Pembroke is noted for its vintage port.

P E O P L E. For its size Pembroke, which at its foundation in 1624 absorbed the fourteenth century Broadgates Hall, has a long list of distinguished men. It seems to have been particularly active in the eighteenth century, a century which all guide book writers of Oxford seem to despise.

Broadgates Hall

John Pym (1584–1643), Parliamentarian.
George Peele (1558?–1597?), Dramatist and poet (and at Ch: Ch:).
Sir Fulke Greville, Lord Brooke (1554–1628), Poet.
Francis Beaumont (1584–1616), Poet.
Sir John Beaumont (1583–1627), Poet.
Rev. Edmund Bonner (1500?–1569), Bishop. Tried Cranmer.
Sir Thomas Browne (1605–1682), *Religio Medici*.
Dr. Samuel Johnson (1709–1784). "Even then he was delicate in language, and we all feared him." (Oliver Edwards an undergraduate of his time.) "I have heard, from some of his contemporaries, that he was generally to be seen lounging at the College Gate with a circle of young students round him, whom he was entertaining with wit. . . ." (Bishop Percy, Ch: Ch:). Considered lectures a survival of mediaevalism. Enjoyed Oxford and revered it.
William Shenstone (1714–1763), Poet.

" . . . he continued his name in the book ten years, though he took no degree. After the first four years he put on the civilian's gown, but without showing any intention to engage in the profession." Dr. Johnson's *Life of Shenstone*.
Sir William Blackstone (1723–1780), Fellow of All Souls'.
Rev. George Whitefield (1714–1770). "It being my duty, as servitor, in my turn to knock at the gentlemen's rooms at night, to see who were in their rooms, I thought the devil would appear to me every stair I went up. . ."
" . . . I always chose the worst sort of food, tho' my place furnished me with variety. I fasted twice a week. My apparel was mean. I thought it unbecoming a penitent to have his hair powdered. I wore woollen gloves, a patched gown, and dirty shoes. . . ."
"After supper I went into Christ Church walk, near our college, and continued in silent prayer under the trees [for near two hours, sometimes lying flat on my face, sometimes] kneeling upon my knees . . . till the great bell rung for retirement to the college, not without finding some reluctance in the natural man against staying so long in the cold." *A Short Account of God's Dealings with the Rev. George Whitefield*, 1740. Made friends with the Wesleys.
Rev. Robert Stephen Hawker (1803–1875), Poet. Eccentric and amiable tractarian Vicar of Morwenstow, Cornwall.
Charles Hawtrey (1858–1923), Actor.

S T. P E T E R - L E - B A I L E Y. See New Inn Hall Street.

St. Peter's Hall.

See New Inn Hall Street.

ST. PETER'S-IN-THE-EAST. An ancient church and archaeologists' paradise hidden away beyond St. Edmund Hall and shaded by trees from New College Garden. A vaulted Norman crypt with cushion capitals is beneath the chancel. The church itself suffered, like all Oxford churches, a violent "restoration" towards the end of the last century, when alabaster, stained glass, Caen Stone and the rest decked it here and there. The chancel vaulting has St. Peter's chains carved in stone crawling across it in a fine lumbering way, marking the structural lines and bravely trying to achieve a pointed arch. The east window has pretty glass.

ST. PHILIP AND ST. JAMES, the cathedral, as it were, of laburnum-shaded North Oxford. Architect, G. E. Street, 1860–1866. "Tasteful and elaborate", *Alden's Oxford Guide*. See North Oxford.

PORT MEADOW. A level stretch along the Isis, west of the town, flecked by sail between Binsey and Godstow. Owned by the Freemen of Oxford since Domesday.

POST OFFICE. An 1880 attempt in the Meadow Buildings manner, recently made refined Tudor inside.

PUSEY HOUSE. An outpost of Catholicism (Anglican) in St. Giles'. Founded in 1880. This is a most successful effort

THE CRYPT OF ST PETER'S-IN-THE-EAST. IT IS NOW TIDIED UP.

in Modern Gothic and was designed by H. Temple Moore. The chapel should certainly be seen for its graceful interior proportion. The idea of it may have come from J. N. Comper's Chapel of St. John's Home in the Cowley Road (1906).

The Queen's College.

BUILDINGS. "Remarkable in their way", an 1870 clergyman historian describes them. But to us, the High Street front of Queen's remains the most satis-

factory composition in all that curve of variegated styles. Most delicate of all is Nicholas Hawksmoor's cupola (1736) over the entrance, with a statue (by Sir Henry Cheere) of Queen Caroline, George II's wife, inside it. Hawksmoor is accused of "heaviness" in his building. This cupola refutes the accusation.

The transforming of Queen's from the usual mediaeval college to its present magnificence started in 1671 with the Williamson Building, opposite St. Peter's-in-the-East. Wren is said to have had a hand in this structure which is now enlarged out of its original compact dignity. Wren may have had something to do with the library (1693–1696), the next Renaissance work in the college, but it is probably Hawksmoor's work as is the rest of the college (various dates from 1709–1736).

On the left across the front court or quad is the chapel, begun in 1719, and which took thirteen years to complete. Complete it still remains, with the contemporary woodwork, Thornhill ceiling of the Ascension, altar piece with copy of Corregio's *Notte*, wrought iron, plaster work, sixteenth century glass by Abraham Van Linge, touched up by one of the Price family in 1717, marble floor and apse. There is almost too much excellence, for the glass, except on a very bright day, takes away from the quality of stone, marble, plaster-work and painting.

The hall is even more impressive than the chapel, despite the windows by Sir Reginald Blomfield. Notice the decoration of the huge barrel-vaulted ceiling, the marble chimney piece and proportion of panelling in relation to the height of the room. Notice the ingenious terminations to the ends of the hall, reminiscent in style more of Wren than Hawksmoor. The college is summoned to dinner by a trumpet.

The library is most impressive. Because Queen's is a classical building it gets fewer visitors than other colleges. The library, therefore, is not usually open to the public. A little interviewing is needed. It is worth all your trouble to see. The under part was originally open but is now filled with an overflow of books. Pass out into the Fellows Garden in order to view the west front which has recently been refaced. Notice the leading and size of the windows and the delicate central ornament of the whole block. The interior has been overcrowded with furniture and additional bookshelves during the nineteenth century. But the proportions of the whole room remain undisturbed. These are so distinguished, the width of the passage between the bookcases is so neatly balanced, the height of the bookcases so carefully con-

Trinity College.

The University Museum, 1855–60.

sidered, that the whole room has the satisfying correctness of a neatly solved mathematical problem. The cases have carving ascribed to Grinling Gibbons. The ceiling is by "Roberts" (I am unable to find any information) and the spaces in the central panels seem to have been filled in later in the eighteenth century.

In the Common Room is a portrait of the time of Henry V.

PEOPLE. Any guide will tell you of the New Year's day custom, which goes back to 1341 when the college was founded, and of the Boar's Head on Christmas Day.

The college has a north of England connection and was noted in the past for Earnshaw types.

John Wycliffe (d.1384), stayed at the college three times. In 1374–1375 occurs this in the Custus domorum "Item pro stramine ad cooperiendam latrinam Wyclyf ijs". "Item mulieri trahenti idem" "Item de x d. solutis uni tegulatori super latrinam Wycliffe", &c. (McGrath *History of The Queen's College*.) Henry V probably stayed at Queen's, the Black Prince less probably.

William Wycherley (1640–1715), left without a degree, having been reconciled to the Protestant religion by the Provost.

Thomas Tickel[l] (1686–1740), Poet of Kensington Garden and friend of Addison (also at Queen's, but migrated to Magdalen). Though a Fellow, received a dispensation from the Crown not to take Holy Orders (then obligatory), not on account of doubt, but in order to secure government promotion.

Jeremy Bentham (1748–1832). His preserved corpse is at London University, Gower Street. Writer on Jurisprudence. Learned nothing at Oxford except "mendacity and insincerity".

RADCLIFFE CAMERA, whose dome gathers the surrounding spires and towers together like a hen her chicks, was built in 1737–1749 from the munificence of Dr. John Radcliffe (see Lincoln College). The doctor was said to have made twenty guineas a day for years and to have received 1,000 guineas from Queen Mary, William III's wife, and 1,200 from King William. He was no tuft hunter and a decided individualist. He gave money for the Radcliffe Infirmary and Observatory, "Bart's", London, and University College, Oxford, Peckwater Quad and All Saints Church and presented the original Mercury bronze in Tom Quad. The present one is modern.

The Camera was used as a Physic and Natural History Library. It then became the home of the catalogue of the Bodleian.

The architect of this building was James Gibbs, who built St. Martin-in-the-Fields, and St. Mary-le-Stand and St. Peter's, Vere Street, and part of Bart's, London, and the Senate House, Cambridge, and the noble classical block at King's, Cambridge. Of all his work, the Camera is the best and one cannot but admire the courage of an age and an architect boldly building in the style of the time right in the midst of some of the grandest work of past ages. How different from the half-hearted attempts to blend the ancient with the modern which characterize post-war Oxford architecture.

One of the only reasons for welcoming the new Bodleian building is that it may enable the vestibule, or ground floor, of the Radcliffe Camera to be cleared of the bookcases which now clutter it. This circular composition, many-domed, and delicately ornamented, is almost as impressive as the reading room above. Even if visitors do not proceed to the roof and pick out the towers with the aid of the little plan provided, I would advise them all to visit the dome. As an essay in perspective, the lessening coffers ascending to the lantern fill even those who use the room, with wonder. Notice, too, the moulding of cornice and spandrels, the adequate reflected light, the substantial quadruple pilasters. At night the dome is flood lit within. At all times it should be seen on the pretext of ascending to the roof.

"This round building", said Charles Larkyns, pointing out the Camera to the credulous Verdant Green, "is the Vice-Chancellor's house. He has to go each night up to that balcony on the top, and look round to see if all's safe."

RADCLIFFE INFIRMARY, up the Woodstock Road (1759–1770), is a decent classic building by Henry Keene with various additions, Victorian and later. Lord Nuffield is the latest benefactor.

RADCLIFFE OBSERVATORY is now visible to the public. It is the first Greek Revival building in Oxford and one of the first in England and was started in 1772, two years after the appearance of Stuart and Revett's *Antiquities of Athens*. There are delicately moulded cornices inside and the number of windows on the eight sides was designed for the use of telescopes.

The exterior of the building is singularly pleasing. Although two architects worked on it (Henry Keene, from 1772 till his death in 1776, and James Wyatt until

1795), the result is harmonious. Keene designed the house, wings and central part as far as the balustrade. Wyatt added the octagonal tower and left room for the sculpture. The top of this tower may be compared with St. Pancras Church, London (1819–1822), by the Inwoods. Hercules and Atlas who support the ball on the top are by John Bacon senior, the precursor of Flaxman. The reliefs round the top stage of the tower are by J. C. F. Rossi, who also did the reliefs on St. Pancras Church.

The instruments which the Observatory was built to contain have been dispersed.

RHODES HOUSE, in South Parks Road, is a combination of Cotswold Manor and Old Colonial (S.A.) designed by Sir Herbert Baker and opened in 1929. There is a don's joke in Greek in the pavement of the entrance hall about not smoking herbs. I cannot say that it is worth going to see, even if you can see it.

Ruskin College.

Ruskin College was founded 1899. The present building is in Municipal-Queen Anne (1912–1913). The college was founded to provide working men with a chance of living University life. Read Roger Dataller's *A Pitman Looks at Oxford* to judge of the effect on one Ruskin man at any rate. The college is down Walton Street, within call of the tubular bells of St. Barnabas, but certainly unconnected with the Establishment, High, Broad or Low.

THE SCHOOLS. See Examination Schools.

SHELDONIAN THEATRE is guarded on the Broad Street side by seventeen mouldering busts of anonymous gentlemen, on the piers of the wall. The theatre itself (1664–1669) is the first big public work of Sir Christopher Wren. It is certainly not his most beautiful building (the alteration of the roof in 1802 did not improve it), but it is one of his most daring. A model of it was exhibited at the Royal Society in 1663 and caused a sensation which increased when the building was actually erected. John Wallis (1616–1703) was Savilian Professor of Geometry at Oxford when Wren was Savilian Professor of Astronomy there. Both were mathematicians and Wallis invented "a Geometrical Flat Floor", which Wren proceeded to work out in applied mechanics and slightly to vary. The result is that the painted roof inside the theatre is seventy feet by eighty feet and without any visible internal supports. It is composed of short pieces of timber.

For Wren the building was not only a triumph of mathematics but also of antiquarianism, for its plan is based on the Theatre of Marcellus at Rome.

Robert Streater (1624–1680)* painted the allegorical figures on the ceiling, framed in gilt cords, holding back red painted curtains. They are worth close inspection, especially the figure called *Rapine*. Sir Thomas Jackson designed the handsome organ case (1877). The galleries and the room above the ceiling were once used by the Clarendon Press.

* Streater's other work at Oxford was in All Souls' Chapel (now "restored" and the paintings have gone). Horace Walpole quotes a poem by Robert Whitehall (1625–85) on the Sheldonian ceiling which concludes:
That future ages must confess they owe
To Streater more than Michael Angelo.

You are allowed to ascend to the lantern to admire the view.

The front of the Sheldonian which faces the Divinity Schools is a clumsy composition. One feels that Wren was so pleased with his mathematical triumph within, that he wasted no time on external embellishments. The impression one gets is of a flat façade filled up with decoration rather than of three dimensional architecture.

The ceremonies that occur in the Sheldonian are noticed on pp. 21–23.

Somerville College.

Somerville College, founded in 1879, is a collection mostly of Edwardian and post-war buildings between St. Aloysius R.C. Church and the Radcliffe Infirmary. It contains about 150 women students. The library is said by bibliophiles to be very good.

THE TAYLORIAN. See Ashmolean.

ST. THOMAS THE MARTYR is an unexpected mediaeval stone church among the brick red lanes near the station. It was so entirely "restored" (except for the tower) from 1847 (J. P. Harrison) onwards, as to be scarcely recognizable from a Victorian church. The interior is dark with fearful glass, but a good baroque scheme of decoration in the chancel has greatly improved the interior. This church was one of the pioneers of the Oxford Movement.

THE TOWN HALL AND MUNICIPAL BUILDINGS. Pre-war architecture never lacked the courage of its convictions. If a building was to be Gothic, it was as Gothic as possible, and if it was to be Queen Anne it was even more than Queen Anne. To-day architects do not show the same courage. If a building is to be Gothic, it is faintly Gothic, if Renaissance, just a suggestion of a moulding here and there, if it is to be "modern" it is so restrained that by attempting to be "traditional" and "modern" at once, it succeeds in looking like what I have seen of the new Bodleian.

The Town Hall and Municipal Buildings are in the true pre-war tradition. Alden's excellent *Oxford Guide* for 1901, describes the style as "full-blown and luxuriant Renaissance". But the contemporary edition yields to the popular taste and leaves out "full-blown" considering "luxuriant" to be enough, though that façade wriggling with decoration in St. Aldate's, and that great quivering, convoluting, golden Town Hall are none the less the knock-out that they were in 1901.

At the end of the last century Sir Thomas Jackson was popularizing his own style of Jacobethan in Oxford. Mr. Henry T. Hare, a well-known winner of competitions for public buildings, wisely decided to make plans in Sir Thomas's manner, and even more in the manner than Sir Thomas himself. The result was that he won the competition and the present peculiar buildings were erected 1893–1897. They replaced a simple building of 1751 by Isaac Ware.

Trinity College.

BUILDINGS. Trinity looks best from Parks Road where the large seventeenth century gates (there is a legend that these will not be opened until a Stuart ascends the throne) look on to a stretch of grass terminated by the three sides of the Garden Quad (1664, 1682, 1728, 1805). One of the earliest buildings by Wren was part of this quad; but his own work is altered out

of recognition. Unfortunately his great scheme for rebuilding the college, drawings of which exist, was never carried out.

There seems to have been some sort of architectural scheme formed by the Tower over Trinity Chapel, the unused entrance

gates in Broad Street and the Tower of All Saint's Church.

The entrance, in Broad Street, is beside the iron gates whose stone piers are in the Dean Aldrich manner. The lodge is part of some old cottages. Cottages such as these once existed all over Oxford, between the colleges and around them. Now they may only be found here and there in the St. Ebbe's district and in some of the lanes off the High Street. Adjoining the cottages is a typical Oxfordshire manor of early seventeenth century type, called Kettel Hall.

The Anglo-Jackson buildings (1883–1887) round this entrance quad were built by Sir Thomas Jackson. They are his best work in that manner in Oxford and look well between the apple trees.

But all this is unimportant compared with the chapel (1691–1694). The exterior needs refacing. The interior, despite some unfortunate greenish glass (1885) which should never have been allowed, is perfectly proportioned and full of admirable detail. The design is attributed to the joint efforts of Dr. Bathurst (president) and Wren and some would add Aldrich. Notice the screen with its carved angels, the plaster work of the ceiling, the oak seats, the exquisite inlay above the table, the festoons carved by Grinling Gibbons, the glass cases containing mediaeval effigies. The Holy Table here is covered with red velvet which blends well with the dark woodwork and forms an excellent base for the silver candlesticks (alas! on a retable). I hope that the college authorities will not go in for "powder blue" and other *ecclesiastical* colours which would spoil this chapel. The red is perfect.

The east side of the small quadrangle is 1417–1620.

The hall (1618–1620 and later) has not been subjected to the craze for pickling. The panelling is still painted, thank goodness, and a white classic ceiling with a good cornice contrasts well with the painted woodwork.

Near the hall is the small and beautiful fifteenth century Library of Durham College, a monkish foundation which stood on the site of the present college. The woodwork is seventeenth century, the books are mostly of this date and earlier.

A new library built as a war memorial in a classical style, exists east of the chapel. The stretch of grass, which one sees from Parks Road, is bordered by a lime walk and a yew walk, survivals of an elaborate formal garden with columns, a fountain, clipped yews, and maze, destroyed in the nineteenth century.

P E O P L E. Trinity is said to be a gentlemanly, old-fashioned college. I do not know whether the feud with neighbour Balliol still goes on. "Bloody Balliol!" was once a familiar evening yell from the entrance quad of Trinity.

Archbishop Sheldon (1598–1677).

Henry Gellilesand (1597–1636), Protestant and mathematician.

Sir George Calvert (1580?–1632), founded colony of Maryland.

Sir John Denham (1615–1669), Poet of *Cooper's Hill*.

Thomas Lodge (1558?–1625), Poet.

Henry Ireton (1611–1651), signed the warrant of Charles I's execution.

William Pitt, 1st Lord Chatham (1708–1778).

Frederick North, Lord North 2nd Lord Guilford (1732–1792).

Thomas Warton the younger (1728–1790).

"While we, with much sincere delight,
(Whether we publish news or fight)
Like England's undegenerate sons,
Will drink—confusion to the Dons!"*

Rev. William Lisle Bowles (1762–1850), Poet.

Rev. James Ingram (1774–1850), President. Wrote the invaluable *Memorials of Oxford* (1832–1837), first full and illustrated guide book to Oxford.

Walter Savage Landor (1775–1864), Poet. Sent down for firing a shot gun at an undergraduate he did not like.

Rev. John Henry Newman (1801–1890), Cardinal. Evangelical when at Trinity as an undergraduate. Removed to Oriel

Rev. William Stubbs (1825–1901), Bishop and historian. Started as a servitor of Ch: Ch: Fellow of Trinity, 1844–1850.

Sir Richard Burton (1821–1890), shot at the Master of Balliol's watering can when he was watering his plants. Rooted up his flowers and substituted marigolds. Expelled for going to the races.

Lord Davidson of Lambeth (1848–1930), Archbishop of Canterbury.

* *The Oxford Newsman's Verses* for the year 1771.

UNION. A collection of buildings in various manners of the Gothic Revival, dating from 1856 to 1911. The library, with frescoes by Burne-Jones, William Morris and D. G. Rossetti, is interesting. While painting the frescoes, Morris is said to have gone to dine at Christ Church with a slab of blue paint in his hair. The buildings are behind the west side of the Cornmarket. The Union is used by political undergraduates for debating, by old clergymen for sleeping and by others as a wash and brush-up place. Since the nineteenth century (it was founded in 1823), the Union has been the training ground of famous politicians.

A HOUSE ASCRIBED TO VAN-
BRUGH IN ST. MICHAEL'S ST.

University College.

The long not very inspired front curves down the High opposite Queen's College. The buildings are mostly seventeenth century, though they look older, those at the western end being only a few years earlier than Queen's College opposite. At the eastern extremity of the High Street front is a plain, classical block of rooms by Sir Charles Barry (designed 1839), the only work by that great man in a University

town. His designs for Worcester College made in 1837 came to nothing. At the western end is a Tudor revival building (1903).

The three things to see in University College are (1) the glass in the chapel, (2) the vaulting in the two entrances, (3) the Shelley Memorial, and of the three by far the best is the first.

The chapel is dark, the east window (replacing a faded enamelled window given by Dr. Radcliffe) and an inappropriate roof and sanctuary were done by Sir Gilbert Scott in 1862. But he allowed the seventeenth century woodwork to survive in the seats and screen. The windows (except that east window) are by van Linge the younger (1641). The most attractive of these windows is that showing Jonah and the Whale in the north wall. Notice the sea, the hills in the background dotted with trees and houses. Though not the best chapel, University has the best seventeenth century glass in Oxford.

The imitation fan vaulting in the porches of the larger and smaller quads may be compared with that other tour-de-force, the vaulting of the staircase at Christ Church. The vaulting in the smaller quadrangle is ingeniously arranged to give an appearance of uniformity to a rhomboid shape.

The Shelley Memorial (a generous recognition on the part of the college which sent Shelley down) reminds one of a municipal art gallery in an industrial town. The nude figure is by Onslow Ford and the municipal baroque surroundings and dome were by Basil Champneys, 1892 and 1893.

Other buildings in view are the hall, over restored but still retaining a timber roof; the Master's House by G. F. Bodley in the Anglo-Jackson style (1879): the library in the Deane and Woodward style by Sir Gilbert Scott, 1860–1861; the buildings along in Logic Lane in the North Oxford Tudor style by H. W. Moore, 1903.

P E O P L E. The college was endowed and had statutes in the thirteenth century. There was a legend that it was founded in 872 by King Alfred. Mr. Falconer Madan* records how Professor Freeman, the historian, caused a small box of burnt cakes to be presented to the master during the millenial dinner of 1872. A good bust by Rysbrack of King Alfred is in the Senior Common Room. The old practice of waking men in the morning by a blow on the door with a wooden mallet survives here, as at Worcester.

Richard Fleming (d.1431), Bishop of Lincoln and founder of Lincoln College.

Rev. John Potter (1674?–1747), Archbishop of Canterbury, author of *Archaeologica Graeca*.

William Scott (1745–1836) and John Scott (1751–1838), who became Lords Stowell and Eldon respectively.

Sir William Jones (1746–1794), "Oriental Jones". Monument by John Flaxman in chapel. "His college tutors, who saw that all his hours were devoted to improvement, dispensed with his attendance on their lectures,

Oxford Outside the Guide Books (2nd issue 1925).

alleging with equal truth and civility, that he could employ his time to more advantage." *Memoirs of Sir W.J.* by Lord Teignmouth, 1807.

Dr. John Radcliffe (1650–1714), graduated here.

Rev. F. W. Faber (1814–1863), Scholar and Fellow. Hymn writer. Converted to Rome.

Percy Bysshe Shelley (1792–1822). "The ring leader of every species of mischief in our grave walls was Mr. Shelley." In his rooms besides piles of books were electrical instruments, magnets, bottles of chemicals, and an air pump. Published a pamphlet called *The Necessity of Atheism* (1811). " 'Did you write this?' . . . 'Then you are expelled,' said the master angrily, in a loud great voice." See Thomas Jefferson Hogg's *Life of P. B. Shelley*, 1858.

Rev. Arthur Penrhyn Stanley (1815–1881), Dean of Westminster.

Sir Edwin Arnold (1832–1904), *Light of Asia*, etc.

U N I V E R S I T Y   M U S E U M, known as the Parks Museum, is an angry Gothic answer to the Ashmolean in Beaumont Street. The design of Messrs. Deane & Woodward, an Irish firm from Cork, was chosen out of thirty-three sent in for competition. The building was not to cost more than £30,000. It cost twice as much by the time it was finished (1855–1860). The style is Free Gothic. "Ruskin himself gave advice and encouragement, and erected one of the columns with his own hand; it is said that the workmen took it down and re-erected it."* The carving of the outside capitals is by O'Shea, but he does not seem

Oxford Renowned, by L. Rice Oxley, 1925.

to have completed his work. Messrs. Farmer & Brindley worked inside. A rare feeling of fantasy is engendered by the interior of this museum, especially when the iron decorations of the glass roof are glimpsed through the bones of a skeleton, while one's body rests against a Gothic column.

Behind this museum, and approached from it, is the Pitt Rivers Museum (1887) ethnologically interesting but less so architecturally. There is a dried up human head concealed behind a curtain.

Wadham College.

BUILDINGS (1610–1613 and 1694). The architect of Wadham was once said to have been Thomas Holt, to whom is also ascribed the Bodleian Tower of Five Orders, University College and Oriel. The architect may equally well have been William

Arnold. Whoever was the architect, Wadham is a complete college of the very latest phase of Gothic or earliest of Renaissance, whichever you like to call it. Except for a few scattered buildings to the south, it is complete in itself and is remarkable as having not a single ugly or modern building in its make up. It is far the most satisfactory of seventeenth century colleges in Oxford, whether viewed from the South Parks Road, or within the quadrangle dominated by the miniature façade of four orders

between the chapel and hall, or from the garden where the purple grey Burford stone of the fabric rises like a manor house along the grass—a Somerset manor, for Somerset men are said to have been employed in building it. Dorothy and Nicholas Wadham, the founders, were Somerset gentry.

The hall, improved for once by stained glass, has the contemporary (1613) woodwork, tables, screen, panelling and a Gothic timber roof finished with Renaissance pendants. The library over the kitchen to the south has the contemporary bookcases and a famous collection of early printed books and English literature—Shakespeare in the first folio, for instance.

The chapel is upon the T plan, and has an east window by Bernard Van Linge (the elder) made in the garden in about 1621. Other windows by him adorn the chapel, while those in the ante-chapel are mostly of the eighteen-thirties and not inharmonious. The organ case and gallery are by Sir Thomas Jackson, the roof and tabernacle work are by the antiquarian architect, Edward Blore, 1831–1832, who spoiled Nash's front of Buckingham Palace.

No one knows what became of the famous painted cloth below the altar in this chapel. All the eighteenth century guide books refer to it. It was painted by Isaac Fuller (1606–1672) and represented the Lord's Supper and other sacred subjects. "The cloth, which is of an ash colour, is the medium; the lines and shades are done with a brown crayon, and the lights with a white one; which afterwards being pressed with hot irons, causing the damp of the cloth to incorporate with the colours, has so fixed them, as to be rendered proof against a brush when used to cleanse it from dust." Horace Walpole admired this cloth, while despising Fuller's work at All Souls and

Seventeenth century tomb in Wadham College Chapel.

Worcester College, Henry Keene's section, 1776.

Magdalen. I suspect that Blore destroyed the cloth when erecting his own altar, which is one of his best works.

The beautiful garden is near the chapel. A large slice of it has been cut off by Rhodes House, but the garden is still park-like, depending for effect upon trees romantically disposed among the grass. From the garden the tracery of the chapel windows is seen at its best, the last Gothic tracery in Oxford before the Revival. Fifteenth century work in 1611–1612.

PEOPLE. This college was founded in the reign of James I (1610). It had at the beginning a west country connection.

Robert Blake (1599–1657), Admiral.

Rev. John Wilkins (1614–1672), Warden 1648–1659, during Commonwealth, and regarded as the only tolerant warden at Oxford; a founder of the Royal Society. Wrote on astronomy, philosophy, language. "He had above in his lodgings and gallery variety of shadows, dyals, perspectives and many other artificial, mathematical and magical curiosities, a way-wiser, a thermometer, a monstrous magnet, conic and other sections, a balance on a demi-circle, most of them his owne and that prodigious young scholar Mr. Chr: Wren, who presented me with a piece of white marble, which he had stained with a lively red very deepe, as beautiful as if it had been natural." *John Evelyn* [1654, July.]

Rev. Thomas Sprat (1635–1713), Bishop of Rochester. Vice-Chancellor. Friend of Wren and Royal Society.

Sir Christopher Wren (1632–1723),

WADHAM COLLEGE

Savilian Professor of Astronomy, became a Fellow of All Souls. Said to have presented the clock to Wadham which is by the chapel.

John Wilmot, 2nd Earl of Rochester (1648–1680), Poet, &c.

Richard Bethell, 1st Lord Westbury (1800–1873), Lord Chancellor.

Rev. Benjamin Parsons Symons (1785–1878), Warden. Extreme Evangelical, arranged times of chapel services so that undergraduates could not attend Newman's sermon in St. Marv's.

During Warden Symons' reign, the Oxford Positivists started at Wadham—Frederick Harrison, Dr. Richard Congreve, and Professor Beesley. They have been described as Three Persons and no God.

Rev. Samuel Augustus Barnett (1844–1913), Social Reformer.

Rev. William Walsham How (1823–1897), Bishop of Wakefield and Tractarian hymnwriter.

Sir Thomas Jackson (1835–1924), Architect and author.

F. E. Smith, 1st Lord Birkenhead (1872–1930).

In 1880 the whole college was sent down because of a "rag".

WESLEY MEMORIAL CHURCH. See New Inn Hall Street.

Worcester College.

BUILDINGS. In the days before bicycles and motor-cars, this college was known as Worcester College, near Oxford, and as "Botany Bay", because of its remoteness. Before Beaumont Street was built the nearest approach the college had to Oxford

was across Gloucester Green and through Friar's Entry, a passage next to Elliston & Cavell's. Beaumont Street was built between 1828–1838 and is the only piece of late

Georgian town planning in the City of Oxford. It makes a graceful curve from St. Giles' and opens up Henry Keene's excellent front of Worcester College (c. 1759). Possibly owing to the arrogant scorn poured upon the classic buildings of Worcester by every Oxford guide book, the Fellows have not dared to remove the revolting creeper which ruins the appearance of this front. They have recently restored the ornamental stonework and would do well to complete their good work by removing the creeper. The creeper is a late Victorian introduction. It would be a kindness on the part of an undergraduate out for a "rag", to saw off this creeper at its roots. Let him make two incisions, one directly above the ground and the next about six inches above the first incision. If he then removes the intervening wood, the creeper will die and Worcester will be restored to dignity.

When you enter Worcester College from Beaumont Street, look at the small entrance to your left and notice the stone staircase which curls up to the library. It is reminiscent of Wren's gallery staircase at the Chapel at Greenwich. You step out from the porter's lodge on to what is the noblest entrance prospect of any Oxford college, a piazza which surveys the good classic buildings on the north side by Henry

WORCESTER COLLEGE, THE PROVOST'S LODGINGS

Keene (1776), and the ancient remains of Gloucester Hall on the south which are level with the sunk lawn and frowned upon, with some justification, by Keene's north block upon its grassy bank. Those old irregular buildings to the south, on your left, which stretch down one side of the quad are on the site of the oldest college buildings in Oxford. They are a series of separate cottages built for monks who came up to Oxford from their abbeys between 1280 and the Reformation. The monks were Benedictine and each cottage was built by an abbey as a *mansio* for its students. Some of the arms of the abbeys to which each cottage belonged are carved over the doors. There were once even more of these cottages at Worcester, but they were destroyed in the eighteenth century. The irregular appearance of these remaining cottages is especially noticeable from the garden (the barge

boards are c. 1830) and the group they form above the flower beds is the subject of countless water colours.

The garden is the thing to see at Worcester. It was laid out in 1827 in the fashionable landscape manner by the Rev. Richard Greswell (1800–1881), a pioneer educationalist. True the lake, lawns and trees seem a little begrimed by the adjacent railway, but it is possible to turn with one's back to the railway and to look across the lake to where the Provost's Lodgings shows its delicate garden front among trees. The effect is that of a remote country house.

The Provost's Lodgings (c. 1760) are like other classic work at Worcester, by Henry Keene, architect of the Radcliffe Infirmary (q.v.), and the lower part of the Observatory (q.v.) and the Fisher Building at Balliol.

As you return from the garden you will

notice how handsome is the great block of buildings by which you entered the college. It has an early eighteenth century appearance, because it was originally planned by Dr. George Clarke, a benefactor to Worcester College (see All Souls) in 1720. Keene did not take on the work of completing the block until 1746 and it was not finished until 1784, eight years after his death. The range of windows, above the piazza, lights the library, a plain galleried room containing a magnificent collection of drawings by Inigo Jones. The chapel was all too re-decorated in the eighteen-sixties by William Burges, an eminent Gothic Revivalist, not much good at what he thought was a Lombardic-Renaissance style.

Mr. Rice Oxley* notes that owing to a certain lack of humour in the arrangement of Burges' inscriptions round the chapel, the word "God" appears, isolated, over the Provost's seat. The hall too suffers from similar, though secular, decoration.

PEOPLE. Worcester College was founded in 1714 by a Worcestershire baronet. Before that date it was known as Gloucester Hall and from 1692–1705, Dr. Benjamin Woodroffe, the Principal, had tried to turn it into a college for members of the Greek church, a church which even in those days was connected with the high church party of the Church of England.

* *Oxford Renowned* 1925.

WORCESTER COLLEGE, BEAUMONT STREET FRONT, LATE EIGHTEENTH CENTURY

Its history between the Reformation, when the Abbey cottages became empty, and the Greek College, is chequered.

Gloucester Hall

Richard Lovelace (1618–1657), Poet. Anthony Wood says he was "then accounted the most amiable and beautiful person that ever eye beheld".

Robert Catesby (1573–1605), Romanist conspirator.

Thomas Coryate (1577?–1617), Traveller and writer.

Sir Kenelm Digby (1603–1665), Diplomatist, naval commander, author.

Worcester College

Samuel Foote (1720–1777), Actor and dramatist. Forfeited his scholarship because of insubordination. When reprimanded by polysyllabic provost appeared carrying a large dictionary to look up the long words.

Thomas de Quincey (1785–1859), Smoked opium as an undergraduate. "I neglected my dress habitually."

Henry Kingsley (1830–1876), Novelist, brother of Charles.

Rev. John William Burgon (1813–1888) wrote *Lives of Twelve Good Men*, useful and excellent book for its light on Oxford. Won Newdigate with poem containing line "A rose-red city half as old as time."

Charles Henry Olive Daniel (1836–1919), Provost. Revived seventeenth century typography.

THE SPIRIT OF THE GOTHIC REVIVAL.   PART OF THE SCREEN OF EXETER COLLEGE CHAPEL
BY SIR GILBERT SCOTT, 1856–59

NOTES
ON SOME OXFORD NOVELS

THE ADVENTURES OF MR. VERDANT GREEN. By
CUTHBERT BEDE (The Rev. Edward Bradley). *Blackwood.* [1853].
In the old tradition of story telling. A "picaresque" novel with the
"picaresque" extracted; and consequently a Victorian idyll, guile-
less and parsonic and to us unreal. Many line drawings in this
book are taken from Verdant Green and were drawn by the
author.

JULIAN HOME—A Tale of College Life. By FREDERIC W.
FARRAR. *Black.* [1859].
Here the University is a certain *Camford*; which is neither one
thing nor the other.

TOM BROWN AT OXFORD. By T. HUGHES. *Macmillan.* [1861].
Arnold-ism at the University. The preface is dated 1861.

THE HYPOCRITE. By C. RANGER-GULL. *Greening.* [1898].
Has an amusing Oxford section. Here we have a very bad young
undergraduate, with an angel's face. Miles away from dear old
Keddy. (See below). He is a real bad egg, this one. "These three
men were bound together by many an orgie (sic), many a shady
intrigue and modest swindle." "Gobien sat down on the chair,
and pulled her on to his knee" (*she* was, of course, a barmaid).
He ends up by committing suicide. Rather a bad advertisement
for his university—but then, he was getting on towards the '90's.

SANDFORD OF MERTON—A Story of Oxford Life. By BELINDA
  BLINDERS. Edited by Desmond F. T. Coke. *Simpkin.* [1903].
  The genuine article. It is all excellent fooling and fun.

THE COMEDY OF AGE. By DESMOND COKE. *Chapman & Hall.*
  [1906].
  A very odd story. Whole-time Oxford and a novel. We have the
  pitiful plight and sorry spectacle of an old don whose feelings
  for a young undergraduate caused him to try to be a youth again
  and mix with his juniors as an equal.

BARBARA GOES TO OXFORD. By BARBARA BURKE. *Simpkin.*
  [1907].
  Barbara is a visitor to Oxford—an admiring and expectant
  visitor—but mainly—where the human element is concerned—to
  senior Oxford. There are amusing descriptions of dons and quite
  impressive ones of senior common rooms.

KEDDY—A Story of Oxford. By H. N. DICKINSON. *Heinemann.*
  [1907].
  A very charming story about dear boys; delightful to maiden
  aunts with nephews up at Oxford. There are "bad influences" in
  it, and "dark pages", but Keddy's the right stuff inside all right
  and comes up smiling and out on top in the end. The maiden
  aunts are reassured.

ZULEIKA DOBSON, OR AN OXFORD LOVE STORY. By
  MAX BEERBOHM. *Heinemann.* [1911].
  First class.

SINISTER STREET. By COMPTON MACKENZIE. *Secker.* [1914].
  The Oxford Section.
  Only "Book Three" of the four books relates to Oxford. "Book
  Three—Dreaming Spires." But that section is a classic in itself,
  where Oxford novel-writing is concerned.

SONIA. By STEPHEN MCKENNA. *Methuen.* [1917].
  Has an interesting section on Oxford; but it is much more than an

Oxford novel. Its milieu (the Oxford bit) is very aristocratic and Christ Churchy—just before the War, in the good old days.

A CITY IN THE FOREGROUND—A Novel of Youth. By GERARD HOPKINS. *Constable*. [1921].
About my favourite Oxford novel. On the *serious* side. It gives "North Oxford" beans. One feels, a *Balliol* book.

PATCHWORK. By BEVERLEY NICHOLS. *Chatto & Windus*. [1921].
Oxford just after the War, or the elect of Oxford, rather, just after the War. An account of B. N.'s attempt to revive the Dreaming Spires and make Oxford what it was in *Sinister Street*.

THE OXFORD CIRCUS—A Novel of Oxford and Youth. By HAMISH MILES and RAYMOND MORTIMER. *Lane*. [1922].
An at times delightful burlesque or parody of previous serious novels, such as *A City in the Foreground* and *Patchwork*. Rather on the long side.

MOST LOVING MERE FOLLY. By PAUL BLOOMFIELD. *Hodder & Stoughton*. [1923].
Early portrait of post-War Oxford.

OXFORD ET MARGARET. By JEAN FAYARD. In French. [1924].
Entertaining and seen from a French angle by a young man who was being pulled in two opposite directions—by France, on the one hand, by Oxford, which appealed to him quite intimately, on the other.

HARVEST IN POLAND. By GEOFFREY DENNIS. *Heinemann*. [1925].
Has a chapter on Oxford in his rather extraordinary, and presumably immature book.

LAUREL AND STRAW. By JAMES SAXON CHILDERS. *Appleton-Century*. [1927].
A most flattering idealization of Oxford by a naïf 'way back American. Would that it (Oxford) were as exciting as he makes

out! He, American-like, idealizes English Oxford and English lords in one and the same breath. A hero, if there ever was one. "I'd go to hell for that guy" says the protagonist, meaning the dean of his college. A *don*-hero, too; Dio mio! ! Its "English slang" is grand.

NEAPOLITAN ICE. By Renée Haynes. *Chatto & Windus.* [1928]. Oxford life in the *Women's* Colleges this time. Quite curious reading from the curious male's point of view; but immature in parts, bordering at times on badness (aesthetically). Women undergraduates, if one may judge by this one, appear to be kinder to dons (the male dons, at any rate), than the men. The hero of this book is actually a crusty middle-aged don—but there is no comedy of age this time. The young thing gets him in the end.

OTHER MAN'S SAUCER. By Keith Winter. *Heinemann.* [1930]. Has an Oxford *Section*. It will go down or not according to people's tastes.

MAKING CONVERSATION. By Christian Longford. *L. Stein* with *Gollancz.* [1931].
Contains a masterly description of an Oxford love affair.

MY BONES WILL KEEP. By Maurice Richardson. *Collins.* [1932].
This is certainly not an Oxford novel; but M. R. brings in the place at a certain stage in his hero's career. It is an "underground" Oxford he describes. An Oxford of pubs,—not colleges.

STORM IN OXFORD—A Fantasy. By Tangye Lean. *Cobden-Sanderson.* [1932].

ACORNED HOG. By Shamus Frazer. *Chapman & Hall.* [1933]. Another premature attempt by an undergraduate while still up.

LITTLE VICTIMS. By Richard Rumbold. *Fortune Press.* [1933].

AN OXFORD TRAGEDY. By J. C. Masterman. *Gollancz.* [1933].

GAUDY NIGHT. By Dorothy L. Sayers. *Gollancz.* [1935]. Good Senior Common room portraits.

INDEX OF NAMES MENTIONED IN THE ARCHITECTURAL TOUR

Where the same name appears in the list under two separate colleges, it follows that the person mentioned belonged to one college as an undergraduate and transferred to another as a graduate.

Index